For Dan

Elees gm

Stephen

THE LAST LAMPLIGHTER
a Soho education

Stephen Fothergill

THE LAST LAMPLIGHTER
a Soho education

Drawings by Peter Saunders

London Magazine Editions

First published in Great Britain 2000
by London Magazine Editions
30 Thurloe Place, London SW7 2HQ
Copyright © 2000 Stephen Fothergill
ISBN 0–904388–83–2
Set in Monotype Ehrhardt by
Rowland Phototypesetting Ltd
Printed in Great Britain by
St Edmundsbury Press Ltd
both of Bury St Edmunds, Suffolk

A CIP catalogue record for this book
is available from the British Library

Paul Potts and *Georgia on my Mind* were first published
by *London Magazine*

CONTENTS

Preface · vii
Soho Claims Me · 1
A Conchie's War · 10
Dressing and Roadwork · 28
Paul Potts · 40
Tambimuttu · 54
Jackie · 74
Some Soho Characters · 94
Lamplighting and Georgia on My Mind · 130
Postscript · 143

PREFACE

Some months ago in the French House in Soho one of the regulars referred to me as 'seriously Soho'. She had in mind perhaps the impressive fact that I had been haunting Soho for nearly 60 years. I thought 'Seriously Soho' would be as good a title as any for this book in which I recall various Soho people I met in the 40s and 50s. However, different ideas prevailed, relating to my other activities in those years.

Much of my behaviour in this period was undoubtedly idiotic. Were I to meet my younger self today I do not think I would like him very much, though I might concede that he had a certain entertainment value.

Where time and place were concerned I sometimes had to employ some guesswork and, life being a chaotic sprawling affair, make an occasional alteration in the interests of tidiness. In essence, though, the book is truthful.

S. G.

Soho Claims Me

During my bleak, clerking years in the City before the war I dreamed of escaping to a colorful bohemian world of poets, painters and artists' models. I had read about such a world in various books that included *The Death of A Hero* by Richard Aldington and *Of Human Bondage* by Somerset Maugham. I indulged in a fantasy existence in which I inhabited a garret in the Latin Quarter of Paris, wrote witty stories with a Socialist message, attended wild bohemian parties and conducted a tempestuous affair with a Spanish flamenco dancer. I had an alternative fantasy of a less frantic nature in which, possessed of a private income, I idled away my days in the Café Royal distributing witty epigrams in the manner of Oscar Wilde. It is small wonder that my work suffered as a consequence of these exotic imaginings.

During my incarceration in the City I fell in love, oddly enough, with a tiny, bespectacled typist who worked for the Prudential Assurance. But Eveleen was pretty, bubbly and unselfconsciously sexy. It has to be admitted however, that she was something of a chatterbox, though she had a posh, musical voice that was most appealing. She was incapable of telling a fib of even the most trivial kind. A staunch

Conservative, she believed wholeheartedly in the British Empire and had a low opinion of lesser breeds, whom she described as lazy and irresponsible. My political views were then naively idealistic. We had numerous arguments that sometimes degenerated into full-blown rows.

Her mother had been a fanatical suffragette and had undergone a short term of imprisonment for attacking a bobby with an umbrella. Despite carrying Eveleen at the time she went on a hunger strike and had to submit to the horrors of force feeding for which she plainly deserved scant sympathy.

When Eveleen was a mere toddler she deposited her in a convent in Eastbourne and more or less forgot about her. Eveleen's father had been equally indifferent to her existence. At the start of the holidays she witnessed the joyous departure of the other girls for their respective homes while she had to face the cheerless prospect of staying behind in the convent.

The pacifist views I then held were the cause of much friction between Eveleen and me. It had been the famous *Daily Express* book of photographs of life and death in the trenches during the Great War – frightful images of corpses rotting in mud – that turned me into a pacifist. I became an active member of the Peace Pledge Union attending meetings regularly and stuffing anti-war leaflets into unnumerable letter boxes.

I once took part in a demonstration outside the RAF base at Farnborough on the occasion of an annual air display. I carried a placard on a pole showing the image of a woman in black clutching a baby and staring up at the sky apprehensively. It was, in fact, a blown up photograph taken during an air-raid in a town in Spain, where a civil war was then raging. There was no other demonstrator in sight and I stood there feeling horribly isolated and vulnerable. It occurred to me that I might be assaulted by a loony patriot with a hatred of pacifists. However, nobody even stopped to engage me in an argument.

I often used to go to Speakers' Corner on a Sunday afternoon to listen to the soapbox orators. The one I most admired – indeed he was then something of a hero to me – was Donald Soper, who later became Lord Soper. A youngish, handsome Methodist minister, he proclaimed in a stentorian voice his passionate faith in socialism and pacifism based on the teachings of Christ.

Over the years Lord Soper continued to mount his soap box every Sunday, fair weather or foul, and proclaim his unchanging Christian beliefs. Still a fan of sorts, I sometimes went down to Speakers' Corner to observe him. I saw him for the last time just a few months before he died. By then he was 95 years old and, crippled by arthritis, held forth from his wheelchair. I went along with the politics but not the religion. He was well-informed, vigorous, jocular and charismatic. However, many of his arguments, as I realized years later, had shaky foundations. He tended to believe what he wanted to believe. A touch of arrogance, moreover, caused him on occasions to dismiss the views of polite hecklers in a brusque, even brutal fashion. He attracted huge crowds in those days and there were lively exchanges and much good humour.

I also enjoyed listening to Bonar Thompson, a gentle, humorous cynic, who wore an old black hat and a tired-looking suit. Born of Irish parents and raised in Manchester, he spoke in the soft accents of that city. He chose to expatiate on the absurd foibles of mankind, which he did with wit and charm. At his core burned an ardent love of Shakespeare. He once confessed that he could not read or hear the name of the Bard without experiencing a tingle in his spine. Unlike Soper, he did not draw large crowds, a fact he appeared not to resent. Nor did he ever decry his ebullient idealism.

He had been a conscientious objector in the First World War. Patriotic ladies were then in the habit of prowling the streets in search of able-bodied young men in civilian clothes to whom they presented a white feather. He was once accosted by a member of that ferocious tribe. 'Why are you not in uniform, young man?', she demanded. 'Because there's a war on, madam', he replied.

Making collections of money in Royal parks was prohibited by law as he used to inform his audience at the end of a meeting. He added, however, that he would presently station himself outside the park gates in Tyburn Way, where he would be happy to receive donations from anybody who had enjoyed his oratorical outpourings. 'To the gates, then!' he would cry with a histrionic gesture. 'To the gates!' He would descend from his soap box and make a slow dignified exit from the park. I would sometimes follow him to Tyburn Way and there shyly slip a half-crown in his hand and thank him.

It was at one of his meetings that I met Captain John Macnamara, a Conservative MP. He was tall, thirtyish and immaculately dressed. He had started up a conversation and, somewhat to my surprise, invited me back to his flat for tea. On our arrival – he lived in Holland Road – we were greeted by a handsome Austrian youth, who was staying with him. During tea, in a rather ill-mannered fashion, I attacked the policies of the Tory government. The Spanish Civil War was then raging. I was pleased to learn that John was not one of those Tories who regarded General Franco as a Christian gentleman and that he supported the Loyalist government. As an uncompromising pacifist I was opposed even to a just war. I suggested that the possibility of the Loyalists losing the war was a powerful argument in favour of passive resistance. John responded with a burst of laughter. As I was leaving, he invited me to dine with him in his barracks the following week.

I felt uncomfortable during the meal in the officers' mess. A problem arose, moreover, when an officer stood up to propose a toast to the King, since I was a fanatical republican in those days. As a member of the choir at St Paul's I would resolutely refrain from participating in renditions of the National Anthem. Now blind panic seized me. I gulped down the remains of my glass of wine, rose to my feet, stared with mock incredulity at my empty glass and pressed it awkwardly to my lips. The whole thing was an abject shambles, though I doubt if anybody noticed my ludicrous little pantomime.

Early one evening a week or so later John picked me up in his car and took me down to the House of Commons, where he installed me in the debating chamber. But the proceedings were dull and there were no famous faces in evidence. Within half-an-hour, however, I was reclaimed by John, who led me through endless corridors to his office. There I met Harold Nicolson, a benign vision in wool and tweed, and Guy Burgess, an intense young man attired in a sports jacket and baggy flannels. John and Harold went off together, leaving Burgess and me alone. Burgess talked about John's commitment to the preservation of the British Empire and of his own whole-hearted endorsement of this. Significantly, he did not mention John's views on the conflict in Spain. It was an excellent performance. Burgess, of course, was then spying for the Soviet Union.

He invited me back to his flat for supper. We made our tortuous way to the street outside, where he hired a cab to take us to Sloane Square. He interrupted the journey to dive into a delicatessen and buy a roasted chicken, something of a luxury in those days. He thought I might like to hear a recording of *The Marriage of Figaro* which he had just acquired. As I reclined on a sofa sipping a glass of wine the bustling sounds of the overture filled the room. Burgess sat down beside me and after a while asked me if I was queer. I told him, rather apologetically, that I was not. After a while I made an excuse and departed. I did not see him again nor John for that matter. John achieved the rank of Colonel during the war. In 1949 he was killed in action in Yugoslavia. His death affected Nicolson deeply as he recorded in one of his diaries.

It was about this time that I became a passionate devotee of Sir Thomas Beecham. I shall never forget my first Beecham concert, which took place at the Queen's Hall, later to be demolished by the Luftwaffe. His orchestra then was the London Philharmonic. However, my initial impression of this famous conductor was far from favourable. I observed a portly, stiff-necked personage with a goatee beard making his slow, majestic way to the podium and wondered doubtfully if he would be capable of inspiring an orchestra to play with vigour and spirit. Having ascended the podium he bowed gravely to the audience and then turned round to converse languidly with the first violinist. He eventually deigned to pick up his baton and then lowered it when he noticed a young couple taking their seats in the front row of the circle. He regarded them for several moments with a marked air of displeasure and then enquired in haughty drawling tones if they had settled down and were now quite comfortable. They nodded nervously. Having turned to face his musicians, he raised his baton and whipped it down fiercely. The orchestra launched into a rendition of the National Anthem that can only be described as electrifying.

Soho Claims Me

Towards the end of the piece Beecham took a step back and then lunged savagely at the percussionist who responded with a drum roll that shook the foundations of the building. At the conclusion of this extraordinary performance three or four members of the audience broke into unrestrained, indecorous applause.

The titles of the musical offerings that followed escape my memory but the shattering impact on me of Beecham's genius is totally unforgettable. I emerged from the Queen's Hall that night in a state of dazed exultation.

Having fallen under Beecham's spell I attended as many concerts of his as I could in the next few years. I especially liked to sit behind the orchestra at the Queen's Hall and watch the maestro doing his stuff at close quarters. What most impressed me about his music-making were its wild demonic aspects. At times, indeed, he unleashed elemental forces of a truly awesome nature. I once attended a concert given by Beecham and the LPO at, oddly enough, an art deco cinema in Croydon, in which one of the works was Borodin's gloriously barbaric *Polovstian Dances*. At the climax of one of the dances a woman sitting in the front stalls, apparently overcome by a mixture of terror and excitement, let out a piercing scream.

His style of conducting was eccentric, to say the least. When he required a *ppp* he would hold his baton horizontally in his left hand, place the forefinger of his other hand against his lips and hiss fiercely. When the music was strongly rhythmic he would do a kind of brisk stationary march on his heels. Sometimes he would stamp violently and utter loud whoops as if urging on a football team. Occasionally his baton would fly out of his hand and into the orchestra. (Two or three spare batons lay on his music stand). On one occasion he accidentally scooped up the music parts of the first cellist who had to stop playing in order to retrieve them from the floor.

At that time I used to indulge in fantasy conducting, a pastime that has always been surprisingly common among otherwise sane members of the male sex with a passion for symphonic music. I based my style, naturally, on that of my musical hero, savage stampings, loud whoops and all. I had even gone so far as to purchase a baton at Boosey and Hawkes, an embarrassing experience.

Alone on a Sunday afternoon in the flat I shared with my father I was conducting my radio, which was blasting out music of a frenetic kind, when there was a loud knocking on the front door. I opened it to find myself confronted by Gert, the stout Cockney lady who inhabited the flat below. 'What a bleedin' row', she protested angrily. 'I was 'avin' a lay down and you nearly made me fall off me bed'. I suppose I should have made a mock, grandiloquent response to this outburst, à la Beecham. Thus: 'Madam, the fact that I failed to transfer you from your bed to the floor means that I was giving a performance of a markedly inferior nature, which grieves me deeply'. Or something of the sort. Instead I apologized sheepishly and promised not to repeat the offence.

The outbreak of war more or less coincided with my dismissal from the firm of coal exporters for whom I had been working for a couple of years. Their action had been fully justified and long overdue for I had been a highly incompetent employee. It seemed that I was incapable of tethering my ballooning mind to the ground during office hours, making awful mistakes in consequence. I did not bother to look for another job since my age group would soon be liable for national service. However, I found my weekly visits to the local employment exchange to pick up 17 shillings rather humiliating and envied Eugene Decker,

Soho Claims Me

the Belgian actor, whom I sometimes encountered there, for his gay insouciance, whether real or affected.

About this time I was introduced to Soho by Selby Wilkinson, an intellectual accountant from Sunderland, who had been a fellow lodger in a guest house in West Kensington. (Years later Selby published a book about the aftermath of the mutiny on the Bounty in which he maintained that Fletcher Christian had secretly returned to England).

I suddenly found myself in a feverish world of artists, musicians, writers, actors, flamboyant queers, prostitutes, café philosophers, layabouts, wild debutantes, villains, Hyde Park orators, street buskers and dedicated eccentrics of various kinds. It all seemed to me incredibly romantic and exciting. Even the dingiest dive seemed magical to me.

A Conchie's War

Shortly after the outbreak of war the Prudential Assurance for whom Eveleen was still working was evacuated to Torquay and she spent the war years there. As a consequence I now saw very little of her. Our relationship, in any case, was beginning to crumble owing to our lack of compatibility. The crumbling process was accelerated by a local caterer called Percy who doted on her and tried to persuade her to marry him. He eventually succeeded and after the war they settled down in a cottage cum bakery on the outskirts of Exeter.

I first met Adolph Schmidt, a German refugee and a lecturer in art, at the beginning of the war. In his native country he had made no secret of his utter loathing of the Nazi regime. On one occasion he had confronted a group of school children, who were marching down a street chanting anti-Semitic slogans, and given them a severe dressing down. A friend of his warned him that the Gestapo were hot on his trail and advised him to flee the country, which he did. Possessed of lean good looks, and a proud bearing, he was brutally honest and entirely lacking in social graces. We used to visit art galleries together and sit around in working class cafés where he expatiated at great length on art in a heavy, emphatic manner that could sometimes be oppressive.

One evening we visited a young composer, Stanley Bate, and his Australian wife Peggy, who was also a composer. (Her professional name was Peggy Glanville-Hicks). They lived in a street off Church Street, Kensington. Adolph dominated the proceedings with an impromptu lecture on Impressionism. Half way through it he broke off to visit their lavatory, where he urinated memorably with the door wide open.

Stanley was handsome in a fleshy sort of way, and affected a superior manner. Peggy was small, slight, tough and very nice. Their flat seemed to me wonderfully civilised in contrast to the dowdy lower middle class surroundings in which I had grown up. I have a vague recollection of white walls hung with modern paintings, curtains in fresh primary colours and art deco carpets. A grand piano dominated the sitting room.

Stanley had studied under Vaughan Williams and been greatly influenced by his music. But he was also fascinated by the music of Stravinsky whom Peggy regarded as a malign influence on him. She believed that Stanley was an essentially romantic English composer and should stay with his roots. Stanley was passionately devoted to composing and there was absolutely nothing else he wanted to do or was prepared to do. However, the country was at war, and his age group would soon be liable for conscription. He decided to register as a conscientious objector when the time came. He told Vaughan Williams of his intention. The older composer, who had served in the ambulance corps in the Great War, advised him to abandon the idea lest he alienate public opinion and thus damage his musical career. He also said he thought a tribunal would consider his desire to devote

The Last Lamplighter

himself solely to musical composition insufficient grounds for exemption from national service.

Some weeks later Stanley and Peggy emigrated to the States and settled down in New York. There, among other things, he composed a symphony, which received a performance from Sir Thomas Beecham, another émigré, and the New York Philharmonic Orchestra.

After the war Stanley returned to England, though Peggy remained behind in New York. Sadly, his resurrected musical career in England failed to blossom and he found himself dogged by financial problems. Friends of his urged him to seek a teaching post in some musical college or other but he resolutely declined to do so. One day he was found dead in his bath. His friends drew the obvious conclusions, although the findings of the coroner's court were inconclusive.

Towards the end of '39 I received my calling up papers and registered as a conscientious objector. My father thought that I should find a job on the land as a means of improving my chances of gaining exemption from military service. I needed gainful employment in any case. Somehow or other I found a job on a pig farm in Hampshire. I cannot honestly say that I enjoyed mucking out pig sties and filling troughs with evil smelling swill. Moreover, I missed Fitzrovia badly, though I was well aware that many Fitzrovians serving abroad were missing it even more than I.

I appeared before a tribunal on a bleak wintry morning in February. My initial nerves disappeared, however, as soon as I began to answer questions lobbed at me by members of the tribunal. I even found myself enjoying these exchanges in which I passionately defended the policy of non-violent resistance. If German soldiers marched through our streets, I declared recklessly, they should be greeted with cups of tea. This would demoralize them completely. Members of the tribunal exchanged broad grins and conferred with one another for a few moments. Then the chairman informed me that they had unanimously decided that my pacifist views were sincere and ordered me to continue working on the land.

Cups of Tea Conchie. This headline appeared that afternoon on the front page of the *Evening News*. Below the headline my idiotic words were quoted in full. On the following week-end the *Sunday Express* carried an article by Beverley Baxter, a famous reactionary journalist, in which he referred contemptuously to a pansy pacifist who would fight the Hun with cups of tea.

Shortly afterwards I went down with a bout of 'flu which lasted for several weeks. I lost my job on the pig farm and returned to London. In April, thanks to the Peace Pledge Union, I found a job on a potato farm in Jersey. We were a team of five, all of us conchies. Our sole task was to heave into the back of a truck clusters of potatoes that had been dug up by a large mechanical fork. The work was back-breaking and we toiled for 12 hours every day. On cloudless days the sun roasted us. From time to time we heard the booming of guns on the French mainland.

France soon fell. The British government lacked the military resources to defend the Channel Islands and had with the greatest of reluctance to abandon them to their wretched fate. I should have stayed behind and greeted the German invaders with cups of tea but in the event I returned to England. I had at least prevaricated for a few days and the boat I boarded was the last one to leave for England before the invasion. I never knew what happened to my conchie workmates, all of whom stayed behind, but they were almost certainly sent to Germany to work in factories.

At Southampton station I was walking towards the platform from which trains departed for London when I was accosted by a bulky middle-aged man in a grey suit and brown trilby hat, who asked me quietly but authoritatively to accompany him to a room nearby. As we sat at a table he studied my identity card and then began to shoot questions at me. What was I doing in Jersey, where was I going, what was the nationality of my parents, where did they live and so on. Then he opened my suitcase and examined the contents which included a few letters. He took especial interest in a lengthy epistle from Adolph, who had emigrated to the States, in which he described his first impressions of the country. However he finally closed my suitcase and told me I could go. I asked him why he had singled me out for interrogation. 'Because you walk like a German', he said.

In those days I had an idiotic habit of imitating the perambulatory style of people I admired. Thus it was from Adolph that I acquired my 'German walk'. This had supplanted my occasional impersonations of Sir Thomas Beecham's stiff-necked, majestic tread. At a later period I used to mimic Laurence Olivier's brisk, martial swagger, in which raised thrusting elbows were an important feature. Unfortunately my elbows rose higher and higher with the passage of time until I resembled some strange bird about to take flight. Eventually I reverted to walking the Fothergill way, whatever that was.

Back in London after my short term of hard labour in Jersey I was struck by the large number of people in uniform walking about the streets. In Soho pubs everybody was talking about the apparent inevitability of a German invasion in the near future. One afternoon I went to a cinema where a *Movietone News* consisted mainly of an interview with Clem Atlee, the Deputy Prime Minister, who, haggard and unshaven, warned the nation to be prepared for the worst.

I found work on a small potato farm in Oxfordshire. We

were a team of two, my fellow spud-picker being the painter Bryan Winter, who like me, was a conchie ordered by a tribunal to work on the land. Years later he was to hold annual one-man shows in a gallery in the Bond Street area. Now, however, he had little time or energy for painting, which depressed him deeply. Possessed of handsome features that were slightly marred by acne scars he was a kindly man with a gentle sense of humour. Nor surprisingly, he found me something of a figure of fun.

Years later he reminded me with a chuckle of a certain bleak, rainy afternoon on the potato farm when he had noticed that the sack of potatoes I was dragging along behind me had a hole in the bottom of it. He commented on the fact that it was leaking potatoes at the rate it was receiving them. I was feeling unusually bored, miserable and apathetic that afternoon. 'I don't care', I burst out and carried on regardless.

Work on the potato farm came to an end and I found employment with the Thames Conservation Board. I became a member of a gang of four, my mates being working class locals, and we toiled on a stretch of the river near Bicester. Clad in rubber waders and armed with shovels, we cleared the bed of the river of accumulations of mud and debris. Our hands entered the water constantly which was highly unpleasant in cold weather. We also cut back trees and bushes close to the river and made bonfires of the risings. My mates took a dim view of my being a conchie and virtually put me into Coventry. The foreman, a youngish man who was awaiting his call-up papers, positively loathed me. As we were sitting around in our hut one afternoon munching sandwiches and downing mugs of tea he suddenly declared with considerable vehemence that all able-bodied young men should be prepared to fight for their country. 'In that case',

I said, playing the Clever Dick, 'you must approve of all those able-bodied young Germans who are fighting for their country'. He glared at me menacingly. 'Shut your bloody trap' he snarled, 'or I'll throw you in the fucking river'. This effectively ended any further exchange of ideas on the subject.

Near the hut lay a sawn-off section of a tree trunk. After our midday snack the foreman ordered me to carry it to a clearing a hundred yards or so away. I managed to shoulder the massive object only with the greatest of difficulty and then staggered resolutely to my destination, where I dumped it with a gasp of relief. On the following morning however, I woke up with a severe pain in my back. I had sprained a ligament and as a result was off work for a couple of weeks.

One freezing January day I contracted frost bite in my left hand and had to give up my job. When the hand had recovered I tried to get into the Auxiliary Fire Service but failed the Army medical to which applicants had to submit. I decided to return to London and offer my services to Civil Defence.

My admirable intentions, however, were put on hold for a few weeks when I met Kate Obermer in the Fitzroy Tavern on my first day back in London. She was an attractive forty-year-old with an appealingly husky, chain-smoker's voice. A shameless extrovert she had verbal style and a robust sense of humour. I felt drawn to her irresistibly.

She had been married to Hubert Ross, the famous music critic. They had thrown numerous parties, at which, a whisky in one hand and a cigarette in the other, she sometimes held court in her bath. After their divorce she had married an American doctor whose name she now bore.

We spent the night in the flat of a friend of hers. Neither of us had a permanent address and during our brief affair slept all over the place. I was completely under her spell and followed meekly wherever she led. Our sole source of income was the alimony she received from her husband and since we spent most of our time in pubs we were often broke and hungry.

Anna Wickham, the poet, put us up for a few nights in her house in Hampstead. She was a big, ungainly woman with a moustache. She habitually wore a heavy curtain, a shapeless mass held together by a length of rope. One morning I woke up to find an old Army rifle propped against the wall close to my pillow. This was Anna's way of expressing her disapproval of my pacifism.

One evening Kate and I took a tube train to a remote suburb where a female acquaintance of hers, from whom she confidently expected to borrow a few pounds, was living. Kate had spent her last penny on the fares. We reached the house in question after a long depressing walk through suburban streets. 'She'll probably put us up as well, darling' said Kate as she pressed the front door bell. The door was opened by a middle-aged woman who stared at Kate for a moment and then exclaimed: 'Oh God, no, I can't, goodbye'! Then she hastily closed the door. 'How absolutely sick-making', declared Kate and lit a cigarette.

We began to trudge through deserted streets in what we hoped was the right direction for the West End. After an hour or so Kate complained that her feet were killing her. It was a cool spring night and anti-aircraft guns boomed in the distance. We came to a halt outside a builder's yard where a shed offered the possibility of sanctuary for the night. Hopefully we scrambled over the wall but found the door of the shed locked. However, there were panels of thick glass in the door. Feeling like a common criminal, I picked up a brick and smashed one of the panels. Then I shoved my arm through the jagged gap, found a key in the lock and turned it. A work bench in the middle of the room served as a bed while a ragged overcoat that had been hanging from a nail in the wall provided us with a surrogate blanket. During the night I had to keep retrieving the garment from the floor. It was the coldest night I have ever experienced. As daylight began to creep into the shed we decided that it would be prudent to make ourselves scarce. Oddly enough, I cannot remember how we managed to find our way back to town. (Kate had that effect on me, as I was beginning to discover).

This gypsy existence was exhausting enough in itself but, in addition, I had to endure constant lack of sleep owing to Kate's insomnia, which she insisted on sharing with me. At night I was kept awake most of the time by her relentless chatter, frequent demand for sex and violent fits of coughing. I had not know at the time that she was secretly sniffing cocaine, which probably accounted for her hyperactivity. It might also have accounted for her paranoia which manifested itself one evening in the Fitzroy. We were sitting at a table when she suddenly urged me in a dramatic whisper to lower my voice. Indicating the wall behind us she hissed: 'Hidden microphones, darling!'.

I ended the affair clumsily but she soon found another boy friend. It had been fun at times and I shall always remember how she would address me occasionally as Stainless Stephen and erupt into husky laughter.

Ann Meo, then an ambulance driver in the Civil Defence, put me up for two or three weeks in her flat above the Express Dairy in King's Road, Chelsea. A hefty, good natured young woman, she had inherited the dark, handsome looks of her Italian father. (Years later she became head of the BBC's sound archives). She had an eclectic collection of records, which she allowed me to play on her gramophone. Her boy friend, an officer in the Royal Navy, was away at sea. Our relationship was quite proper. However, Dylan Thomas, a drunken, disheveled figure, sometimes turned up after the pubs had closed and spent the night with her.

He was not a pretty sight the following morning with his blood-shot jaundiced-looking eyes and ashen complexion. At pub opening time he would make his unsteady walk to the Six Bells just down the road and there embark on a boozing session with a Chelsea character known, for some reason, as James the Shit. Significantly, perhaps, he lacked three or four front teeth in his lower jaw.

In this period I was completely broke and went hungry most of the time. Ann had been unable to help me to get into Civil Defence and so I presented myself hopefully to various CD stations in West London. This entailed traipsing through endless dusty, bomb-scarred streets to the occasional accompaniment of air raid sirens. But I failed to get taken on by any of the stations. At one of them I was told that conchies were *persona non grata* there and at another that applicants with a Grade 3 medical card were ineligible for service in Civil Defence. A chance meeting in a pub led to my finding a job as a full-time fire watcher with an advertising agency in the Fleet Street area.

I shared a room at the top of the building with two other fire-watchers. The room contained three chairs, a table and three canvas beds. My fellow fire-watchers were working class, not unfriendly, and hopelessly addicted to Woodbine cigarettes. One of them was an affable old man who would slowly and laboriously read his copy of the *Evening News* as if he were committing every word to memory, the other a wizened fifty-year-old with extraordinary sad eyes.

We reported for duty at 6 o'clock every evening. Provided

The Last Lamplighter

no air raid was in progress we turned in around midnight, having divested ourselves of jackets, sweaters and footwear. Even on a quiet night the snoring and coughing of my room mates made it impossible for me to sleep. When sirens sounded an alert we scrambled out of bed, dressed, struggled into overcoats and donned tin helmets. Then we lurched bleary-eyed up the stairs to the flat roof where a small shed contained our fire-fighting equipment. Searchlights probed the sky, anti-aircraft guns boomed and falling shrapnel struck hard surfaces with a sound unpleasantly reminiscent of pistol shots. Single planes with their lethal load flew high in the sky above us looking strangely lonely and vulnerable.

Sometimes we heard only the sinister sound of their engines. One night we saw a plane tumbling out of the sky in flames, a spectacle greeted with cheering from fire-watchers on neighbouring roofs.

Some weeks later we saw a plane flying low over roof tops and assumed it was mortally wounded and out of control. What we had actually seen was our first flying bomb. Hitler had launched his V1 missile attack on London. Our camp beds and so on were moved to a room on the ground floor but my fellow fire-watchers spent their nights in the basement of the building opposite. We all imagined that conventional raids had ceased for the time being. I caught up on desperately needed sleep that was only interrupted briefly by the odd bang in the night.

Before long V1s acquired the nickname of doodle bugs. They were fearsome contraptions but you could at least hear them coming and they announced their murderous descent by cutting off their engines, thereby giving potential victims a chance to take cover. V2s, their successors, which were simply rockets loaded with explosive material, merely gave a brief shrill whistle before impact. The resultant explosion, when heard at a distance, brought to mind the sound of a hammer whacking a tin tray.

One day at the Royal Exchange I attended a lunch-time piano recital given by Solomon. Afterwards I was strolling past St Paul's Cathedral when I heard the distant sound of an explosion and saw a black cloud rising in the sky to the west. I continued walking until I reached Aldwych where a scene of horror confronted me. The dead and dying lay everywhere. Many victims of the explosion, however, had merely been struck by flying glass. Dazed and bewildered, they wandered about aimlessly or merely sat on the ground. Some of them were weeping. Ambulance workers dashed about coping as best they could.

One Friday evening I picked up my wage packet as usual but learnt that the head of the agency wanted to see me in his office. As I entered the holy of holies the occupant regarded me with an expression of extreme hostility and informed me brusquely that he no longer required my services. He said he did not like my kind of person but declined to elaborate. I departed in a somewhat bemused condition. I could only conclude that he did not like conchies and had just discovered that I was a member of the despised tribe, something I had not revealed when I applied for the job. On the other hand he might have thought that I walked like a German, though I think that I had abandoned this perambulatory style by then.

Months earlier I had fallen heavily for a poet called Barbara Norman. She had black, lustrous hair, tragic brown eyes and a straight soldierly back. She favored navy blue sweaters and skirts and sensible shoes. She smoked Woodbines, those cheap, acrid-smelling, highly carcinogenic cigarettes so beloved of the working class in those days. Occasionally she treated herself to a packet of Sobranies.

The Last Lamplighter

Blessed with a modest private income – she would have hated to have had a substantial one – she lived in a tiny bed-sitter in Chelsea. She frequented local pubs and cafés, armed usually with a note pad which she filled with scraps of poems and little drawings. Her tense, electric personality utterly fascinated me.

She could trace her ancestry back to the Black Prince. Her maternal grandmother had been the illegitimate daughter of Empress Eugènie, the wife of Napoleon III. Barbara's father, an army man and amateur potter, was the first cousin of Montagu Norman, the governor of the Bank of England in the 1930s.

Barbara registered as a conscientious objector and was granted complete exemption from national service by her tribunal. She was sometimes abused in pubs for her pacifist stand by people outside her bohemian circle. Some of her detractors saw her smoking Sobranies with their black wrappers and imagined she was a dope fiend. As a consequence she was banned from one of her favorite pubs. We spent a night together, a drunken giggly affair, but when I met her in a pub on the following day I had the feeling, a mistaken one as I learned years later, that she had taken against me. I began to avoid her in future, thereby ending a relationship that had hardly begun. I realize now I was suffering from a rejection complex, which meant that I unconsciously wanted her to reject me.

For a time I worked as a telephonist, oddly enough in view of my love of booze, at the National Temperance Hospital in Hampstead Road. During busy periods I would feel positively persecuted by the calls that poured in relentlessly. When the switchboard was relatively quiet, however, I would seek to relieve the boredom of it all by answering calls in various accents, Cockney for instance, or Glaswegian, but only if the calls were of a fairly trivial nature. One evening after the completion of my shift I was prevailed upon by a nurse to help her carry a shrouded corpse on a stretcher down to the mortuary. As we descended the stairs, with myself in front, the feet of the dead person began to push against my back, a distinctly eerie experience.

I ought to have soldiered on at the hospital – rockets were then raining down on London – but I accepted the tempting offer of a temporary job as a spot operator at the famous Bedford Theatre in Camden High Street. (The theatre had been renamed the New Bedford when it became a 'palace of varieties' in the 20s). Walter Sickert had frequented the theatre in the Edwardian era, as many of his paintings testify, when it had been a music hall. It survived the Second World War unscathed, only to be demolished in the 60s by property developers.

Working in a room above the gallery, I enjoyed chasing artistes about the stage with my spot, which could be adjusted to cover a line of chorus girls or merely the face of a vocalist. At my elbow was a box of color slides: green for Irish tenors, pink for female warblers, blue for 'adagio dancers'. white for comedians and so on. Whenever possible I synchronized my changes with the beat of the music. At the end of a show, for instance, when the artistes marched on from the wings as the pit band belted out a lively tune I kept the stage bathed in a pink light, and on the final climactic chord whipped out my slide to hit the stage with a dazzling white light. Leon Cortez, the famous bandleader, who put on a show while I was there, once praised my nifty spot lighting.

The audiences consisted mainly of working class women, who liked to sing along with a vocalist when he or she was performing a familiar, well-loved melody. However, they did so softly and almost reverentially, which I found very moving.

After the job came to an end I found another one, though not as a spot operator, at the New Theatre, which was later retitled the Albery. The Old Vic Company, whose cast was headed by Laurence Olivier, Ralph Richardson and Sybil Thorndike, had taken up temporary residence in the theatre.

My job consisted of tending two small lamps attached to a mast on the opposite prompt side of the stage. To reach them one had to climb up a wooden ladder to a small platform referred to as a perch. In the prompt corner there was another perch whose occupant, then an art student, also had two small lamps in his charge. Colour slides had to be changed and lighting levels established. Sometimes we had to snap on or snap off our lamps or gradually build or fade them. We worked from plots and received our cues in the form of red and green lights from the stage manager in the prompt corner. The perches were certainly an excellent vantage point from which to see the shows. Indeed, they were almost as good visually as a box in the theatre. (A royal box, in my case, as my perch was on the opposite, prompt side).

One of the plays in the repertoire was *Richard III*, in which Olivier gave a terrifying performance as Shakespeare's misshapen monster. In the final scene Olivier achieved a kind of elemental grandeur as he staggered about the battlefield, a lonely, abandoned figure, bawling out the desperate refrain, 'My kingdom for a horse!' I shall never forget the scene in *Peer Gynt*, another play in the repertoire, in which the eponymous hero (Ralph Richardson) gently rocks his mother (Sybil Thorndike) in her rocking chair as her life gradually fades away. Her mournful intonings and Grieg's sombre music, played by the pit orchestra, were extraordinarily moving.

A Conchie's War

Since the theatre only needed me for shows my earnings were rather meagre. They went mainly on rent and draught beer and I was usually broke by the middle of the week. During one of those penniless spells I subsisted solely on omelettes composed of flour and water. Since I had no fat of any kind in which to fry them they all had a burnt flavour that at least made them less boring. On hungry days I traipsed around pubs and cafés in the hope of borrowing half-a-crown from one of the regulars. At that time this weighty coin, for which I had a great affection, circulated freely among penurious Sohoites.

I was then living in a partly furnished room in Maple Street in Fitzrovia. Philip O'Connor mentions this room and its occupant in his *Memoirs of a Public Baby*. (I figure in the book as Ernest). '... an incredible room. I saw an immense mahogany bedstead with a narrow camp bed within it in which the eccentrifying Ernest slept in dirty white flannels'. He fails, however, to mention the cracked window panes, caused by the descent of a rocket on Whitfield Street, and the upright piano standing in a corner of the room. The instrument had been loaned to me by a middle-aged couple who had no room for it in their temporary flat in London.

I had received piano lessons as a child and been compelled to play pieces with titles like *Elfin Revels* and *Pixie Frolics*. Now I plodded every day through two early sonatas by Beethoven and a Chopin nocturne. However, I seemed unable to master any of them. During my fire-watching days I had had a few lessons from a piano teacher called Mr Sidebotham. On one of those occasions, as I was struggling through a simple prelude by Bach with my eye glued to the score, my piano teacher asked me if I suffered from defective eyesight. I had to admit that I did not, which was rather

The Last Lamplighter

humiliating. The owner of the piano eventually reclaimed it and I was pianoless for several years.

The house I lived in was owned by old Mendelsohn who also owned two bric-a-brac shops, one in Berwick Street and the other in Rathbone Place. He had dank gray hair surrounding a large dome and wore shabby clothes that looked as if he slept in them. Despite his unprepossessing appearance he was an habitué of the Café Royal, where he sat every evening at a marble-topped table near the entrance. In his house there was a small room crammed with bric-a-brac in which he slept at night. He had a young daughter, Dinora, a shy lovely creature who worked as a showgirl in night clubs. She eventually married a young peer with a passion for motor racing.

After the Old Vic season ended I worked for a couple of weeks in old Mendelsohn's shop in Rathbone Place. It was opposite the Wheatsheaf, the bohemian pub where J. Maclaren-Ross, the novelist, monopolized anyone within earshot night after night at one end of the bar. Most of the bric-a-brac, pretty dismal stuff, was displayed in a haphazard fashion on tables in the street. On one occasion old Mendelsohn reprimanded me severely for indicating to a potential customer a chip on the base of an unappealing Victorian dinner plate. During those two weeks I failed to sell a single item.

For a brief period I worked in a kitchen in the Corner House in the Strand. My sole task was to empty sacks of potatoes into a metal revolving drum where they were attacked by fierce jets of water and then expelled to thunder down a chute to a receptacle in the kitchen below. I worked alone in the room and the desperate boredom of it all impelled me to burst into strident song from time to time as a form of emotional release. My vocal repertoire consisted of operatic arias and themes from favorite symphonies. The revolving drum and bouncing potatoes made a tremendous din and so I was able to let go. On occasion I indulged in a spot of flamenco dancing or something of the sort, which included vigorous hand clapping and vociferous olés. I suppose I had something of a ball at times among those dancing spuds.

However, I bade them farewell in order to have a go at working as a film extra. A casting agency dispatched me to Shepperton Studios where Shaw's *Caesar and Cleopatra* was being filmed. The shooting in question was to take place in the open air. It was August but the weather was unseasonally grey, cold and windy. As a shivering Roman soldier with blue knees I must have looked singularly unimpressive. Certainly the other Roman soldiers who numbered about 200, and clearly suffered from varying degrees of hypothermia, could hardly have struck terror in the hearts of the enemy. Day after day from about six in the morning until eight in the evening we hung about waiting in vain for the Director, Gabriel Pascal, to shout 'Action'. The boredom was excruciating. After five days of this misery I chucked it. I decided that any job, however unpleasant, was preferable to one that merely involved hanging around.

Travelling up to Shepperton by train on my last day I unfolded my *News Chronicle* to learn that an atom bomb had been dropped on Hiroshima. A few days later Nagasaki suffered the same fate, and the Japanese Emperor sued for peace.

Dressing and Roadwork

Before long I found a job as a dresser at the Cambridge Theatre, where a season of ballet was in progress. Oddly, I cannot recall the name of the ballet company or even of the dancer I dressed, whom I shall call Lawrence. In one of the ballets, based on Glazounov's *The Seasons*, Lawrence, as an exotic tropical bird, had to tear about the stage flapping wildly and occasionally leap high into the air. Before he made his entrance I had to get him out of the costume he wore in the previous scene and into the feathery one as he stood panting heavily in the wings. The change had to be accomplished in about ten seconds. One night, in my customary state of panic, I accidentally put his costume on back to front, thereby pinning his arms to his sides. As he stumbled on to the stage he tried desperately to extricate himself from his straight jacket but to no avail. I averted my gaze and kept it averted until the curtain fell. As he tottered into the wings he strove to find adequate verbal expression for his rage and frustration but only succeeded in emitting peculiar strangled sounds.

Before his first costume change he would remove two rings from his finger and entrust them to my care for a few

Dressing and Roadwork

hours. I cannot describe the rings since I gave them no more than a fleeting glance as I slipped them into the right hand pocket of my trousers. One evening, however, as he was changing back into his leisure clothes I dipped into this pocket as usual to retrieve the rings but found to my horror that one of them was missing. Then I discovered that this pocket had sprung a leak. I wandered about the theatre in a desperate attempt to find the missing ring but without success. Understandably Lawrence was very angry indeed but he sneeringly rejected my explanation for the disappearance of the ring. I was summoned to the office of the theatre manager, who subjected me to a brief interrogation. However I think I convinced him that I had not stolen the wretched thing.

A week or so later the ballet season came to an end and in that short period I managed not to inflict further harm on the hapless dancer. I decided, however, to give up working as a dresser.

Les Ballets Russes de Monte Carlo moved into the theatre and I was taken on as a showman electrician. I worked on the prompt side of the stage, my main task being to tend a large lamp on a five-foot stand. These lamps were known as floods.

My favorite ballet was *The Polovstian Dances*, which in fact was a scene from Borodin's *Prince Igor*. These dances were choreographed by Serge Lifar, the famous dancer who was discovered by Diaghilev in the 20s. As the dancers leapt wildly about the stage he would stand in the prompt corner urging them on by dint of stamping savagely to the rhythm of the music and punching the air fiercely. This in itself was an exciting spectacle.

Every night towards the end of the ballet the exit door in the prompt side was opened wide and the stage door likewise.

As soon as the curtain fell for the last time the principal male dancer streaked down to the street where he stood for several minutes panting for dear life.

In *L'Apres-Midi D'Un Faune* a half-naked, portly Lifar gave an hypnotic performance as the mythological creature. The curtain rose on a darkened stage and then my flood, containing an amber slide, began to build on Lifar crouching on a rock. This at least was supposed to happen. On the first night, however, the flood began to illuminate not Lifar but a showman in the flies. The lamp must have received a knock from a descending flap in the black-out preceding the rise of the curtain. I decided not to reset the lamp, which would have been a clumsy, distracting business. All I could do was to await the forthcoming storm which duly arrived as I stood by my flood with my head bowed in shame.

For years I had been cherishing a dream nourished by the writings of Henry Miller, of going to live in Paris. His extravagant praise of the city, indeed, had persuaded me that merely living there was an end in itself. However, his romanticizing of his reckless bohemian existence, which involved being at times broke, hungry and homeless, had for me, naïve soul that I then was, a dangerously seductive appeal. I decided to realize my dream but first I had to knock up some money.

My theatre work allowed me to do another job as well, even a full-time one, and thus I found myself one day demolishing orange boxes with a chopper in a bomb-damaged building in Covent Garden. I had two mates who were engaged in a similar task, the purpose of which I cannot now recall. It probably never occurred to me to wonder what it might be since I was absurdly incurious about everyday matters in those days.

Vanloads of orange boxes arrived throughout the day and

before long I began to feel positively persecuted by the wretched things. I would sometimes kick a box viciously before attacking it with my chopper and hurling at it savage oaths, or rather hurling oaths at it savagely for I am sure they were of a fairly innocuous nature. However, they appeared to shock a middle-aged woman who dropped in occasionally to do the books. She threatened to give up her job if I continued to work there, and so I was given my marching orders.

I had managed to save about £10, and decided to take the plunge. I had heard that coffee was scarce in France and therefore an expensive luxury and so I bought four packets of coffee beans with the fell intention of engaging in a spot of profiteering when I arrived in Paris. (In the event I did not have the heart to demand an exorbitant price for the beans – the potential buyer, a young woman, was obviously of modest means – and sold them for little more than I had paid for them).

Poor, battered London had been dirty, shabby and grey but Paris, which had survived the war virtually unscathed, seemed in comparison amazingly clean, fresh and spruce. There was even a touch of gaiety in the air. (This was the summer of 1947). I loved the way Parisians strolled about the streets in the evening and sat for hours outside brasseries and cafés imbibing glasses of wine. The city then had a distinctive smell that has been described as a mixture of Gauloises, perfume and drains.

I found a cheap tiny room in Montparnasse. The stone floor was uncarpeted and the small window lacked curtains. I only used the room to sleep in.

My favorite haunt was the Dôme, where so many expatriate Americans foregathered in the 20s and where, a decade later, Henry Miller had strutted his stuff. Here I encountered Oliver Bernard, a fledgling poet, and Bruce, his younger brother, who was an art student. When I asked them what sort of time they were having in Paris Oliver said they were drinking and starving. David Sylvester, who later became an art critic, was another habitué of the Dôme. He told me where to find cheap, good restaurants and how and when to tip.

We went to a cinema one evening to see an American movie with French sub-titles. The wise-cracks were untranslatable and we found ourselves roaring with laughter in an otherwise silent cinema.

John Burns Singer, the poet, who died tragically young, was another familiar face at the Dôme. He seemed to live in a constant whirl of poetry readings, private views, literary parties, restaurants and bars. He took me to one of those parties, where I met an exceedingly drunk young American. On learning I was English he scowled at me, suddenly turned green and lurched out of the room.

Before long I began to run out of money and looked around for a job. I found one as a kitchen hand in a small restaurant. My French was limited, to say the least, and communication with the chef in command was extremely difficult. He resorted at times to elaborate mime and angry bellowing. The work was frantic, the heat intense and the atmosphere charged with ill-feeling. The powerful smells of the kitchen clung to my clothes. At night the odours hung about my room.

I toiled for two weeks in that hell hole and then transferred myself to the comparatively salubrious surroundings of a cafeteria in a 'tent city' on the outskirts of Paris. My fellow kitchen hands were three gloomy young Russian giants, who had a smattering of French but spoke mainly in their native tongue. The long hours were profoundly depressing – we started at eight in the morning and finished at eight, or even

Dressing and Roadwork

later, in the evening – but the pace at least was leisurely and there was lots of fresh air.

One of my tasks was to serve meals from behind a counter to the inhabitants of the camp. One afternoon, somewhat to my surprise, I found myself serving Oliver and Bruce. It seemed that they were now eating as well as drinking.

The tent city closed and autumn arrived with a nip in the air. I had learnt that fuel supplies in France were extremely low and did not welcome the prospect of spending the winter in unheated buildings, so I decided to escape to the south, for I was then under the delusion that the south remained warm throughout the year. Marseilles sounded highly appealing but I would have to hitch-hike most of the way.

I set forth one chill October morning with a shoulder bag containing a few basic necessities, a large bar of plain chocolate and a bag of peanuts. I was virtually broke but as a disciple of Henry Miller I felt that this was entirely appropriate.

The first lift I managed to thumb turned out well. The vehicle in question was a comfortable old banger whose owner, a mayor of some town or other, was an enthusiastic Anglophile. He invited me home for an evening meal and put me up in a spare room where I slept blissfully in a feather bed.

The following day was rather less pleasant. I was picked up by a disheveled young man in his sports car which he proceeded to drive in an erratic manner at high speed. He steered with one hand and with the other clutched a bottle of whisky from which he took frequent swigs. I was greatly relieved when he brought the car to a shuddering halt and wished me good luck. I spent the night in a barn where I was kept awake by constant squeakings and sinister rustling noises.

The Last Lamplighter

On the following morning I found myself rolling southwards in a lorry whose driver was taciturn but friendly. He dumped me at the bottom of a steep winding road having lopped off at least 200 miles from my journey. As I was making a laborious ascent of the road a policeman appeared round a bend, stiffened visibly when he spotted me and began to bear down on me purposefully. My scruffy, unshaven appearance and the crew cut I then sported with its suggestion of Devil's Island must have aroused his deepest suspicions. As he started to interrogate me I produced my passport which he examined carefully. Having decided I was not a desperate criminal on the run, he allowed me to continue on my way. Minutes later another policeman appeared round a bend and at once proceeded to descend on me in a markedly determined manner. He scrutinized my passport and then returned it with a disappointed air and waved me on. A hundred yards or so farther on yet another policeman appeared round a bend and the same ritual was enacted. At the top of the hill I had to pass a police station and did so with a fair amount of alacrity.

Later on that day I was trudging along a deserted road when I suddenly became aware of a young French officer marching towards me. I wearily reached for my passport in anticipation of the inevitable questioning that would ensue. It failed to impress him, however, and he ordered me to accompany him to a military camp nearby. I decided not to question his authority. Throughout the ten minute walk to the camp he kept a wary eye on me. A senior officer in the camp examined my passport and then returned it with appropriate apologies.

I continued to trek southwards. Vehicles on the road were few and far between and none of the drivers I waved at was willing to give me a lift, which was not altogether surprising.

Dressing and Roadwork

Darkness fell but I was determined not to spend another night in a barn and simply kept going. As a crimson sun rose on the horizon I found myself, miraculously it seemed, on the outskirts of Marseilles. But I could walk no farther. I lay down on a grass verse by the side of the road and fell asleep instantly.

The sun was riding high in the sky when I regained consciousness. Shamefully aware of people walking past me on the pavement, I struggled to my feet and started to head shakily for the centre of the city. I was now completely broke and very hungry. In spite of this, however, I enjoyed roaming about the streets of this warm-hearted, vibrant, robust city. A fun-fair on the sea front was irresistible, and as I wandered around I found myself hoping to spot a bank note or coin lying among the litter on the ground but had no luck. I spent the night among Arabs in a waiting room on the main railway station. In the morning I emerged from the station cold, exhausted, miserable and, by now, really starving. Feeling utterly defeated, I trailed along to the British Embassy in Marseilles in the naïve hope of raising a small loan to tide me over for a few days and enable me to look around for a job. The young attaché I saw, however, informed me that the Embassy would only be prepared to lend me the price of a railway/boat ticket to England. I told him that I was determined to remain in France. Finally, and somewhat reluctantly, he dipped into his own pockets for a loan of two or three pounds. Shamefully, I never repaid it.

Two or three days later I found a job as a temporary gardener with the American Hospital, which was situated on a hill overlooking the Bay of Angels. However, the job came to an end before long, and by then, perversely enough, I began to experience twinges of nostalgia for foggy London

The Last Lamplighter

streets and Soho pubs. I decided it was time to go home. At the British Embassy in Nice a surprisingly uncensorious attaché lent me on behalf of the Embassy the wherewithal for my journey, plus expenses. Several years later I repaid the loan.

Back in London I moved into a furnished, gaslit attic in North Kensington and shortly afterwards applied successfully for a job as an English teacher at the Berlitz School of Languages in Oxford Street.

One of my students was a French colonel who liked to talk about classical music. On one notable occasion he maintained that Elgar was a minor composer. Deeply shocked, I struggled to find words to express my passionate conviction that Elgar was a very great composer indeed, but somehow the moment passed. Another student of mine was a handsome young Swiss woman with alluring bags under her eyes, who smothered herself in exotic perfume. I would have liked to suggest that we met for a drink one evening in the French but lacked the nerve to do so. I gave one lesson to a Russian engineer. As we were reading aloud a chapter from one of the textbooks that consisted of graded conversations I suddenly found the stilted sentences hilariously funny and succumbed to a fit of giggles. The giggles turned into guffaws which eventually affected the bemused Russian who lapsed into a bout of baritone chortles. The lesson ended in complete shambles.

One morning I had a lively young Chinese student who shot questions at me with the rapidity of machine gun fire. Contemptuously disregarding the obligatory conversational method he concentrated on tricky grammatical problems. On that occasion I was nursing a bad hangover and feeling exceedingly frail. Suddenly I clutched my forehead and uttered an involuntary groan. My relentless persecutor, as I

Dressing and Roadwork

regarded him, told me in concerned tones that he thought I was not at all well and suggested that the lesson come to an end. Then he departed. After this incident the number of students allotted to me decreased noticeably. Soon there were virtually none.

I decided to drop into the New Theatre and see the Chief Electrician. He had once inadvertently put into one of my wage packets a pound over the odds, which I had returned to him, and thus I was in his good books. He said he was willing to re-employ me and a week later I found myself back on my old perch.

In the summer of '49 a re-formed Old Vic company, which included Olivier and Vivien Leigh and which had been touring Australia, took up residence in the theatre. The tour had been a gruelling experience and the company struggled through the rehearsals in a state of extreme exhaustion. Sometimes the rehearsals lasted from 9 o clock in the morning until 11 o clock at night. Although Olivier had assumed the extra burden of directing the lighting effects of a new production of *Richard III* he never once to my knowledge lost his temper or displayed a trace of irritability.

Sitting in the stalls with his lighting plot Olivier could only communicate with us perchmen (perchers?) by means of strenuous lung power and we were only able to make contact with him in a similar manner. As he was bawling out instructions to us one afternoon his voice began to slur and eventually ceased altogether. Overcome by fatigue he had subsided into a deep slumber.

Vivien Leigh, who played Lady Anne in Richard III, missed one performance of the play owing to a sore throat. A terrified understudy stepped into her shoes. During a scene with Olivier she forgot her lines completely and Olivier had to deliver them for her. When it was time for her to

The Last Lamplighter

take a bow at the end of the play she merely stood there looking embarrassed and shaking her head. On Olivier's insistence, however, she reluctantly took a bow, a brief apologetic one, as the audience applauded sympathetically.

After the final performance of the season Olivier threw a party in his dressing room to which the entire company and the stage crew had been invited. For some reason Vivien Leigh sat by herself in a corner looking rather cross but Olivier mingled happily with his guests. Towards the end of the party he made a tour of the room to stop from time to time, raise his glass of wine to guests and declaim, 'Till our next merry meeting!'

My next job was at the Hippodrome, where it was back to lugging a flood about the stage. The show, entitled the Folies Bergères, featured topless show girls who were then required by the Lord Chamberlain to remain utterly motionless in their semi-naked state. A young, zany, hirsute Michael Bentine had a slot in the show in which he did extraordinary things with a chair while uttering wild shrieks.

I rarely drank in the afternoon in those days but on one occasion I had a few drinks in the French pub and then drifted down to the Mandrake Club. I stayed there downing drinks until it was time to go to work for the evening show. By then I was well and truly plastered. However, I managed to stagger down to the theatre where during the first scene change, I reeled about the stage in a state of utter confusion. I was vaguely aware of one of the electricians 'striking' my flood. I heard a voice saying 'Get him out of the theatre for God's sake', and found myself being led to the stage door by the Chief Carpenter and ejected from the premises.

On the following evening I slunk back feeling acutely embarrassed. The chief electrician was a nice man and handed me my insurance card and a wage packet with

Dressing and Roadwork

obvious reluctance. He also gave me a little lecture on the evils of heavy drinking. However, although I enjoyed booze-ups, I was not an alcoholic and knew I would never become one.

Paul Potts

The war against Hitler had started a couple of months earlier and I was sitting with Tony Dickins one afternoon at the bar of the Wheatsheaf in Fitzrovia. My companion's chief claim to fame was his launching of *Poetry London* in the previous year in tandem with a Ceylonese poet called Tambimuttu. He was in the middle of a fervent apologia for homosexuality when a youngish man with receding hair and a hungry wolfish look suddenly appeared at his elbow, greeted him brusquely and asked him if he had half-a-crown to spare. Tony said he was unable to oblige and began to describe the parlous state of his finances. 'All right, all right', snapped the gentleman with the vulpine look. 'So you can't help me.' Whereupon he moved away to seek salvation in another part of the bar. 'Who on earth was that?', I enquired. 'That', said Tony sombrely, 'was Paul Potts. He writes poems with a socialist message and sells them as broadsheets in the streets. The poor fellow always seems to be on his uppers. He's sort of Canadian. Born over there but educated mainly in England.'

Shortly after this little episode Paul, as I later learnt, joined the Army as a volunteer, and I did not see him again for two or three years. Possessed of a healthy loathing of Hitler, he had been keen to make a contribution towards ridding the world of his odious presence. Paul, however, proved to be something of an embarrassment to the Army for he was hopelessly maladroit and neurotically averse to any kind of discipline. In Northern France – amazingly, he was serving with 12th Commando – he broke cover on a couple of occasions to wander about the countryside blithely unconcerned about the proximity of the enemy. He thus endangered not only his own life but those of his comrades-in-arms.

The upper echelons decided that something had to be done about this dangerous idiot. So he was dispatched to London and put in charge of the canine mascot of his outfit. This was hardly Paul's idea of fighting for democracy. Besides, he detested dogs. However, he eventually managed to obtain an honourable discharge from the Army.

It was about this time that I spotted him sitting alone at a table one night in the Swiss pub in Old Compton Street. (It is now a queer establishment called Compton's bar.) The wolfish look, happily, was not in evidence. His hair had receded dramatically since I last saw him, but the noble dome now on display more than compensated for his loss of hair. He had a certain presence, due partly to his clean cut features, candid blue eyes and the aforementioned dome, which brought to mind a high-minded Democratic senator. Or would have done if it had not been for his food-stained clothes and dirty fingernails.

I introduced myself, found that he was disposed to be friendly and, noticing that his glass was empty, offered to buy him a drink. A Guinness was requested and duly obtained. Somewhat to my surprise he downed it in about four seconds. After a while the empty glass seemed to be standing there positively demanding to be replenished. Paul appeared not to notice as he talked about his experiences in the Army. 'Another drink, Paul?' 'No, no, I don't want another drink. Yes, please. More of the same, old boy.' (As I later learnt, he had a predeliction for this upper class term, which I found as incongruous as if he had suddenly donned a bowler hat or produced a rolled-up umbrella.) I took his glass back to the bar to be filled again with the dark, foaming liquid. Paul polished it off before you could say Jack Robinson. I concluded that he always drank in this extraordinary fashion. I eventually got him another Guinness, which suffered the same brutal fate as the others. Then he declared, somewhat unexpectedly, that he would like to give me a meal.

We repaired to an Italian restaurant, where we settled with startling originality for spaghetti bolognese. The helpings were generous but Paul demolished his in two minutes flat. Much of his spaghetti, however, failed to reach its intended destination and lay strewn over the tablecloth. Having smartly dispatched a black coffee, Paul announced quite casually that he was broke. So I had to foot the bill. As we were about to part company outside the restaurant Paul said: 'Can you lend me half-a-crown, old boy? Bus fares, you know, and my entrance fee to the French tomorrow morning.' I duly obliged.

Paul had apparently reverted to his pre-war state of indigence, which was relieved only by his annual grant from the Royal Literary Fund and occasional publication of a poem or an article. It was his wont most mornings to descend on Soho around pub opening time and devote the rest of the day to borrowing half-crowns and cadging meals and drinks from odd bods floating around the area. Those marathon tapping stints must have imposed a severe strain on his nervous system and partly account for his frequent outbursts of hysterical rage.

Paul Potts

I often ran into Paul in various Soho establishments. He was usually ebullient and talkative in a nervy sort of way but sometimes embarked on a prolonged whinge about his awful life. 'I should have been a doctor or an architect', he would moan. 'I should have married and had children and led a civilized life. But I'm a poet, God help me. I never know where my next meal is coming from. I live in a doss house among social outcasts. Bar tenders sneer at me when I enter a pub without any money for a drink. I should have been a doctor or an architect.' And so on.

These plainings were virtually identical. Indeed, the Scottish painter, Robert MacBryde, once compared them, rather unkindly, to an old gramophone record. There was a period when Paul sported an American looking trilby and, during angry denunciations of people who had humiliated him, repeatedly snatched it from his head, which was evidently in an overheated condition, and jammed it back on a minute later.

It seemed to me that having even a mundane job, teaching English to foreign students, for instance, or working in a book shop would have been preferable to his stressful, time-consuming method of surviving. (His lack of qualifications ruled out more remunerative and prestigious occupations.) I should have realized, of course, that his childishly hysterical temperament would have made it impossible for him to hold down a job. However, I cautiously broached the subject one day but he said that he would be worse off financially if he had a job of the kind I had in mind. This disclosure astonished me. I knew that he engaged in a spot of pilfering from time to time but his main source of income was undoubtedly those half-crowns he so assiduously netted every day in Soho.

The victims of his light-fingered activities were mainly

friends whose houses he visited – usually only once. He tended to favour silver cutlery and valuable books. On one occasion he was leaving his host at the end of a dinner party when a book slid to the floor from inside his overcoat. His host recognized it at once, since it was a collector's item. He had noticed that Paul's overcoat was bulging rather strangely. In icy tones he asked him to hand over the other books lurking inside his coat. Three or four were produced and grudgingly returned to their owner. Then, to the astonishment of his host, he asked him for half-a-crown. I do not know how he reacted to this impudent request but I like to think he saw the funny side of it and coughed up.

During the course of some Saturday night bash or other at which Paul was a guest, his host had wandered into the kitchen and found Paul leaving hastily by the garden door. 'Paul', he exclaimed. Visibly startled, Paul spun around to reveal that he was wearing three of his host's best shirts. And there was the bizarre episode of the Radio Doctor's overcoat.

During the forties Charles Hill, a Tory MP, used to give talks on health matters on the Home Service, now known as Radio 4, and thereby acquired the nickname of Radio Doctor. He had a bluff manner that bordered on the absurd. One afternoon he dropped into the Colony Club, where he surrendered his overcoat, a posh one, to the cloakroom attendant. This was Bobby Hunt, an art student, who later became a book illustrator. Paul was also in the club that afternoon, having left his less posh overcoat with Bobby. When he later sought to reclaim it Bobby gave him the Radio Doctor's by mistake. It was a handsome garment which took Paul's fancy. He slipped into it, found it a good fit and made a hasty exit.

An hour or so later Bobby set out in search of Paul clutching an old overcoat that smelled of booze and tobacco. He was feeling embarrassed and angry in equal measure. He found Paul in the French, where he was preening himself, or so it seemed to Bobby, in the Radio Doctor's expensive overcoat. Confronted by Bobby he resolutely declined to hand over the coat in exchange for his own. Finally, Bobby told him in colourful terms what he thought of his outrageous behaviour. Paul responded by calling him a Fascist monster and stalking out of the pub.

But Bobby was determined not to be bested by Paul. He too left the pub and began to follow Paul at a discreet distance as he weaved his way through various streets and alley-ways. He eventually came to a halt outside an Italian restaurant into which he disappeared. Warily peering through the window Bobby was able to discern Paul hanging up the overcoat and then sitting at an unoccupied table. Seizing this golden opportunity Bobby dashed into the restaurant, flung Paul's overcoat over a peg, grabbed the Radio Doctor's garment, made a lightning exit and jubilantly hot-footed it back to the Colony.

Paul had a tendency to let fly at the drop of a hat with deeply wounding insults. As a consequence it was not uncommon to see him sporting a black eye or swollen jaw or cuts on his face or a combination of all of these. Occasionally somebody got in first with a damaging slight but Paul could always top it.

One evening I was sitting with him in an Italian restaurant where he had just assaulted a plate of spaghetti bolognese with the usual unfortunate consequences to the tablecloth. He was craving a cigarette with his coffee but I had none as I was a non-smoker. A Sohoite we both knew was sitting at the next table and Paul asked him for a cigarette.

Bill, young, working class and emotionally screwed-up,

was a lorry driver cum film extra. He drank heavily and had a tendency to wallop people who displeased him. At the moment he was eyeing Paul with extreme disfavour. Finally he said: 'I don't give fags to poncy gits like you.'

'You should go back to the gutter where you belong', snapped Paul, a rejoinder distinctly unworthy of a supposed socialist.

Bill got to his feet and stood over Paul, menacingly breathing beer fumes.

'Come outside, you cunt', he muttered thickly.

'I have no intention of coming outside', said Paul. 'I suppose you want to hit me. Well do it for heaven's sake and then bugger off.'

Bill looked puzzled for a moment. But amour propre prevailed and he duly punched Paul in the face. He raised his fist to repeat the action but thought better of it and lurched back to his table.

Within seconds a large lump had appeared on Paul's left temple but he sat there calmly as if nothing had happened and picked up the threads of our interrupted conversation. Although his head must have been aching badly he made no reference whatsoever to this ugly incident during the rest of the evening.

In later years he adopted the practice of delivering an insult and then adding 'Joke'. Thus: 'I don't know why I'm talking to a dreary little hack like you. Joke.' or 'You're a reactionary monster who ought to be thrown out of Christendom. Joke.' As a consequence he sustained fewer facial injuries.

I was fairly dotty in my early wandering about Soho days, but in time it became clear even to me that Paul suffered from a pronounced streak of madness. So I feel he was not really responsible for much of his shocking behaviour. It was as if his emotional development had been arrested in the cot. Babies, for instance, are unable to distinguish between what belongs to them and what does not, which may well explain why Paul could nick things from friends without experiencing the slightest twinge of remorse. But he was a deeply unhappy man. I would describe him, indeed, as a tortured soul.

It would be grossly unfair not to mention his admirable qualities, for he did have quite a few. He possessed, of course, physical courage. Indeed, he was absolutely fearless. He genuinely hated bullies, though he would sometimes accuse somebody of bullying him when the person in question was merely expressing outrage at his bad behaviour. The practice of verbally abusing and humiliating people was once prevalent in Soho, but if anybody received this sort of treatment in Paul's presence he would fly to his defence with savage invective. He invariably visited friends of his who were languishing in hospital, provided, of course, he had the fare. And he loved to give signed copies of his books to friends – I was the recipient of three. (He sometimes sought to reclaim one of them to give, usually, to an American publisher.) Nobody could have been less of a hack than Paul, for he was incapable of penning a single sentence that did not come from the heart.

'I only want my bus fare', Paul would say as we sat together in the French or wherever at the end of an evening. Then he would add: 'I'll take whatever you give me'. And I would discreetly slip him a bit of the ready. But if I encountered him when he was plush, a rare occurrence, he would gladly bestow on me a few notes accompanied by a mock formal bow and then offer to buy me a double whisky, which I always declined in favour of half-a-bitter. I used to find his lofty mien on these occasions annoyingly condescending until

I realized that he was playing the role of an honourable gentleman discharging an old debt.

I am no authority on poetry, which, for some unfortunate reason, I am unable to enjoy. So I cannot pronounce on the merits or demerits of Paul's verse. Its begetter had no high opinion of it and eventually settled for writing prose, which as it happens, often reads like poetry.

He only published four short books, three of them prose works, which can hardly be described as a substantial body of work, especially as he lived to be 79. However, in view of the sort of life he led this modest output could be regarded as an impressive achievement.

Certain themes dominate his writings: the evil nature of tyranny, whether of the left or right, his romantic socialist faith, Israel (passionately pro), his extravagant hopeless love for sundry eccentric, mostly upper-class women, and his exalted vision of love itself. He also wrote about friends, some of them famous, for whom he had a high regard.

One of these was George Orwell, who is the subject of a whole chapter entitled Don Quixote on a Bicycle in his autobiography *Dante Called Her Beatrice*. He captured the essence of this brave, kindly man with loving acuity. Ignazio Silone once told him that an essay on himself by Paul, which appeared in some literary magazine, was the most penetrating account of his spiritual beliefs that he had ever read. (Paul had visited Silone in his retreat in Switzerland, and, true to form, asked him for a loan. This Silone accorded him after a solemn rummage under his mattress.)

I deeply admire the last chapter in Paul's *To Keep a Sacrament*, which is about Anne Devlin, an Irish skivvy who was arrested by the British Army after the 1803 uprising in Ireland and detained for four years. Throughout this period her jailors tortured, abused and humiliated her in an effort to make her reveal the whereabouts of the leaders of the rebellion with whom she had been consorting. However, in Paul's words, 'she never spoke a comma'.

Somebody once said that Paul could write marvellous sentences but was unable to manage paragraphs. This was too sweeping a judgement but there is something in it. One does feel that Paul was beginning to struggle for breath towards the end of some of his paragraphs. But he did have a way with sentences. Short and pithy, many of them qualify as aphorisms. Occasionally, however, he allowed himself to be carried away by lofty sentiments and as a result produced sentences of a gaseous, hyperbolic nature.

His standards of personal hygiene were never high. He sometimes had an unwashed, unshaven look and his hands were often grubby. However, in his late sixties – by then he was sporting an unkempt, grisly beard – he acquired a body odour that can only be described as dire. He had apparently given up taking baths and seldom washed. He suffered, moreover, from both sorts of incontinence, for which he declined to seek medical treatment. He simply ignored the whole problem and as a result the most appalling accidents happened. But they appeared not to bother him in the least. As he entered a pub a terrible odour rapidly filled the whole room. Gaston Berlemont, the landlord of the French pub, never liked to bar anyone but he could not allow this olfactory assault on his customers to continue. He eventually decided that he would have to present Paul with an ultimatum. With this in mind he took him aside one afternoon. 'It really is too bad, sir', he said reproachfully. 'As soon as you come into the pub my customers leave in droves. You really must do something about this awful smell otherwise . . . well . . . its quite impossible.' Paul muttered something about being bullied and shuffled out of the pub never to return. It seemed

The Last Lamplighter

he was unwilling or unable to relinquish what had become known in Soho as the Paul Potts Smell.

Having now become unwelcome in all his haunts Paul holed up in his Highbury flat, only venturing forth to do a spot of local shopping. A few resolutely loyal friends, most of them women, used to visit him from time to time but had to face scenes of horrifying squalor in which excrement played an important part. Some of them even undertook the heroic task of cleaning his flat, though the fruits of their labour were shortlived.

The horror stories I heard about the squalid conditions of Paul's flat effectively discouraged me from visiting him for some years. Then one day I heard he was receiving home help on a daily basis. So I rang him up one morning to find out if it would be in order for me to drop over later, which it apparently was.

The house was early Victorian like most of the buildings in the neighbourhood. None of the electric bells worked and the front door lacked a knocker. To make my presence known I had to resort to a vigorous demonstration of lung power. There was a muffled shout in response, a window on the first floor was opened slowly and an ashen-faced, heavily bearded Paul peered down. 'Nice to see you, old boy', he said. Whereupon he flung down a couple of yale keys attached to a piece of string. Both the keys and the string were encrusted with dirt.

I entered an uncomfortably warm room, where Paul was lying on a bed. A faint smell of ammonia assailed my nostrils but nothing worse, to my immense relief. A black-and-white television set by his bed flickered dimly and emitted faint sounds. (It stayed on all the time I was there.)

Clad in an old shirt Paul lay on top of the bed with his knee almost touching his chest, which gave him an oddly foetal look. I produced half a bottle of whisky from one of my pockets, having deemed it imprudent to bring a whole bottle, and under its benign influence Paul began to relax and assume a more normal position.

It soon became apparent that this was not the Paul I used to know. His conversation now consisted solely of verbal ejaculations separated from each other by painfully lengthy silences. The old passion and exuberance had vanished. But he was at least compos mentis and, thanks to his hard-working television set, well-informed on global events. He also listened with keen interest to my scraps of Soho gossip.

He was now virtually bed-ridden and depended on a Zimmer frame for slow, arduous excursions to the bathroom and kitchen. I told him I thought he must find this restrictive existence exceedingly tedious but he said this was not the case at all. There were those friends of his who visited him regularly, his charming home help – she even dropped over at week-ends for which, of course, she received no payment from the local council – and his ancient, much loved television set.

His writing life, naturally, was over. Some years earlier he had talked of embarking on a new book to be entitled 'I May Be White But I'm Irish'; however, nothing came of it. Firmly attached as I am to the idea of conking out as noisily and defiantly as possible, I could hardly admire Paul's passive response to the proximity of the Great Reaper. Nevertheless, in view of all those years of hardship and emotional torment he had endured, I could not really begrudge him this closing chapter of life in which, liberated from money worries by the Department of Social Security and cosseted by various charming women, he luxuriated shamelessly in abandoned indolence.

He was touchingly anxious to be a good host but had no

food or drink in the flat. To remedy the situation he asked me to do a spot of shopping for him. On the floor beside the bed stood a large, open tin with coins of various denominations topped by a thick layer of bank notes. (This was ironic in view of all those decades of penury.) He extracted a couple of tenners and gave them to me. I made a list of the things he wanted and set out for the shops.

I returned half-an-hour later laden with various goodies. Having eaten recently I settled for a few grapes. But Paul, lying flat on his back, set about demolishing a bag of peanuts, several bananas, a bunch of grapes, a large slab of nut chocolate and a vanilla ice-cream cone, all more or less at the same time. Before long his beard had acquired splodges of ice-cream, which he made no attempt to wipe away. He occasionally grabbed a mug from his bedside table and took a noisy gulp of lager laced with whisky. From time to time he emitted a loud, prolonged belch.

In the middle of the fray Susan, his home help, let herself into the flat. Youngish and attractive, she somehow suggested a ballet mistress. 'Paul', she exclaimed, 'you know you mustn't eat lying on your back.' Paul merely grunted and continued to noisily scoff his goodies. Susan now issued a command. 'Paul, be sensible and sit up.' 'Oh, do stop bullying me', cried Paul. But Susan kept on insisting that he do her bidding. Suddenly he erupted into a stream of hysterical abuse in which the four-letter word played a prominent role. Susan, however, stood her ground and eventually he calmed down and then, looking exceedingly cross, heaved himself up to a sitting position.

Susan told me later that Paul's practice of guzzling food in a supine position when she was not there had landed him in hospital a few weeks earlier. Lumps of unmasticated food had accumulated in the lower part of his oesophagus and had had to be removed by means of a pump. Much of this detritus proved to be in a rotting condition.

I always turn with dread every morning to the obituary page of 'The Times', where so often I have been informed over the years of the death of a friend or close acquaintance. One morning I found myself confronted on this page by a photograph of Paul. It was taken when he was old and bearded.

His death had been dramatic. Alone in the flat one evening he had been smoking his pipe and accidentally set light to his bed. Neighbours, alarmed by the smoke pouring out of his flat, telephoned for the fire brigade. When the firemen burst into his room he was alive but badly burned, so badly in fact that much of his central nervous system had been destroyed. This meant he was at least experiencing no pain. He indignantly ordered the firemen to leave, an injunction, of course, they did not take seriously. Ambulance men duly arrived. However, Paul, unaware of the serious nature of his injuries, protested vigorously when they transferred him from his bed to a stretcher. They rushed him off to hospital, where he died within a few minutes.

Tambimuttu

I was sitting one evening at the beginning of the Second World War in Coffee an', a bohemian café in St Giles Passage on the outskirts of Soho. The walls of the smoke-filled room were decorated with jazzy murals. A swarthy accordionist topped by a beret was retailing '*Deep Purple*', a sad, evocative tune popular at that time. Much green and brown corduroy was in evidence. Two bearded gentlemen were locked in combat over a chess board at the next table. In a far corner Stephen Spender was talking with a sixteen-year-old Lucian Freud, who wore a trilby hat.

Boris Watson, the bear-like owner of the café, stolidly distributed meals and drinks and cleared tables. He had Bulgarian parents, who rejoiced in the name of Popoff, and was, a trifle surprisingly, an Old Pauline. One night, years later, I saw him strike a man on the head with a metal knife-sharpener. The man staggered from the café bleeding profusely and died later. Boris was charged with manslaughter but acquitted. I once asked Gaston Berlemont, the landlord of the French pub, what he thought of the sanguinary business. He gave a Gallic shrug and said: 'Balkan politics, I suppose'.

Tambimuttu

The chair opposite me had been taken by a strikingly handsome young man with brown skin and a profusion of lustrous black hair. His dark intense eyes proclaimed steely determination and yet, disconcertingly, his slack jaw suggested weakness and irresolution. He was drunk.

'I'm Tambimuttu, you know,' he informed me without ceremony.

Then, raising his voice dramatically, he added: 'I'm known in Soho as the Great Muttu!'

He gave a self-deprecating giggle.

'But my friends call me Tambi, you know.'

Raising his voice again he declared: 'I'm a poet. I celebrate life in all its various aspects: people, music, trees, rain, love, pubs, market places. I've got fire in my belly, you know. I despise intellectual versifiers and their anaemic efforts. I once told Louis MacNeice, you know, that he produced milk-and-water stuff.'

He gave another giggle.

He went on to tell me with the aid of numerous 'you knows' that he was a Tamil from Ceylon, who had come to England in the previous year and launched a poetry magazine, later known as *Poetry London*, with a music student called Anthony Dickins. They had netted many well-known English poets and created something of a stir in literary London.

Tambi scoffed a plate of steak and chips and departed, having invited me to a party he was throwing on the following evening.

Minutes later a bizarre figure entered the café carrying an old bag. He was attired in a black hat, an opera cloak and a brightly coloured cravat. But his most compelling feature was an iron frame attached to his right leg. He clumped over to my table, sat down opposite me and carefully deposited his bag on the floor.

The Last Lamplighter

'I'm Iron Foot Jack,' he announced importantly, 'and oi sells genuine old antiques.'

'And oi'm a bo-yeemian,' he added with tremendous pride.

However, he suddenly grabbed his bag and stood up. 'Oi've just seen an individual over there wot owns a bricky-back shop and oi reckons oi can do meself a bit of good in that direction.'

I wished him luck as he lumbered away.

The party was in full swing when I arrived. Tambi and his wife, Jackie, shared a flat with Jack Diamond, a Labour member of the local council, in a large gloomy building opposite the Fitzroy Arms in Charlotte Street.

Jackie was a tranquil, sweet-natured girl, who, in decorous parlance, would be described as well-endowed. She had been a Girton girl. I also met Stephen Spender. Tall and distinguished-looking, he had melancholy eyes and wild hair. He talked slowly and gravely, enunciating every syllable with care in the manner of a parson delivering a sermon. At that time he and Cyril Connolly were editing *Horizon*. He told me they received vast numbers of poems about masturbation, all of them entirely lacking in literary merit. Presently he left to go on to another party. David Gascoyne, the Catholic poet, sat silently in a corner of the room. Attired in an expensive tweed suit and a bow tie, he had the air of a dandy. But heavy bags under his eyes denoted acute insomnia. A flushed, shrunken Dylan Thomas was also one of the guests. His eyes, like those of Tambi's, proclaimed strength, while his loose jaw gave the opposite impression. He expressed astonishment at my high-speed mumbling, a deplorable habit of mine, and jocularly invited me to recite a poem. I declined, however, to do so. Paul Potts had been standing at his elbow and regarding him with marked hostility. 'So you think I'm a cunt?' he burst out suddenly. 'Who am I to question what the Almighty in his infinite wisdom has ordained,' replied Dylan grandly. Then he lurched off in search of the loo. He returned some minutes later with his flies unbuttoned, collapsed on the floor in the middle of the room and lay on his back breathing heavily. He was entirely oblivious of the fact that his private parts were on display. I hastily averted my eyes to be rewarded by the sight of a handsome, sturdy young woman sporting a beret, who had just entered the room. This, as I later learnt, was Audry Beecham, a niece of Sir Thomas Beecham and one of Tambi's poets. She was a judo expert. On one occasion she employed her skill to good effect when a man attacked her in the street. She simply threw him over her shoulder and walked on.

Also at the party was Eugene Decker, the Belgian actor noted for his portrayals of hammily romantic Frenchmen. We were in Jack's sitting room, which was dominated by a huge, magnificent-looking radiogram. Into it Jack reverentially fed a stack of records from time to time. During a lull in the proceedings Eugene took it upon himself to put on a record he rather fancied. Jack felt that his cherished machine had been violated and sternly rebuked the malefactor.

Tambi had invited an uncle of his to the party. A portly, genial personage, who was on holiday in England, he seemed to be enjoying the strange antics of these natives of Fitzrovia. Suddenly he seized a large brass tray and began to beat out lively Tamil rhythms on it. Tambi responded by launching into a frenzied dance which involved much stamping and sinuous double-joined finger work. At the climax he shouted: 'I'm the Great Muttu, you know.'

I first met Tony Dickins some days later in the Wheatsheaf and found him ebullient, brilliant and quaintly upper middle-class., Under the mistaken impression that I was queer, he

The Last Lamplighter

embarked on a eulogy of homosexuality that contained the names of Plato, Michelangelo and Gide. He went on to describe with shining eyes his years at Cambridge as an undergraduate: music, books, parties, the city itself and unlimited sex of the kind he favoured. I felt he knew, poignantly, he would never recapture the magic and excitement of those years.

Several drinks later we set out rather unsteadily for Coffee an'. Black-out regulations were in force and our only source of light was a sliver of moon. Outside the café I succumbed to a childish impulse to climb to the top of the railings of St Giles Church and relieve my bladder. Having clambered down I found myself confronted by an unfriendly-looking copper. 'Wot was you doin' hup there?' he demanded in the verbal style then favoured by bobbies. 'Peeing in the wind!, I cried lyrically.' Hin that case,' declared my interrogator, 'I will 'ave to charge you with hindecent be'aviour in a public place.' Fortunately Tony intervened on my behalf while I kept prudently silent. His abject apologies for my infantile conduct eventually persuaded the policeman to let me go.

I often encountered Tambi in Fitzrovian pubs where he consumed large quantities of watery war-time bitter, recited poetry, dropped names shamelessly, and reminded us from time to time that he was the Great Muttu.

A penniless friend was Philip O'Connor, the surrealist poet notorious for his witty savagings of people he disliked – nearly everybody – which were accompanied by animal noises and mad, high-pitched sniggers. He and Tambi were drinking together one night in the Wheatsheaf when the latter suddenly declared in a loud voice: 'Some people, you know, are poets some of the time but Philip O'Connor is a poet all of the time.' Philip emitted a shrill whinneying noise.

In the new year Tambi and Jackie moved to a ground

floor flat in Marchmont Street which in those days boasted a fruit-and-vegetable market. However, their marriage was beginning to develop serious cracks. This was not surprising. During the day there was a constant stream of poets and pub acquaintances through their small sitting-room, which also served as an office. In the evening Tambi was out on an extended pub crawl. This was hardly a suitable existence for a young woman who suggested a life of country pursuits.

They would discuss at length the parlous state of their marriage, Tambi being unwilling or unable to change his way of life, and decide finally to separate. Then Tambi would say: 'Let's go to bed, you know.' The suggestion was put into effect and they would make love with unusual zest. The painful decision taken earlier would be forgotten. Some days later they would have another earnest talk about their crumbling marriage and again resolve to separate. But Tambi would again say: 'Let's go to bed, you know,' and so it went on.

One of Tambi's peculiarities was an aversion to shoe-shops. Whenever he needed a new pair of shoes Jackie would go to a shoe-shop in the neighbourhood with whose owner she had an arrangement whereby she picked up half-a-dozen pairs of shoes in Tambi's size and brought them home for his inspection. When he had chosen a pair, she took the others back to the shop and paid for the one he had kept.

One afternoon in his flat Tambi was trying to explain to me the meaning of one of Auden's poems and laughing good-naturedly at my baffled expression. Suddenly there was a knock on the front door. Jackie sighed and rose to her feet in response to a sound she had come to hate. Moments later a tall, strangely beautiful girl with fair hair entered the room. She was coldly aloof, yet the fixed intensity of her eyes suggested that she was a prey of powerful emotions.

Tambi had met her in his bachelor days and instantly

The Last Lamplighter

fallen for her. Soon afterwards they went on a jaunt to Paris where Tambi assumed they would become lovers. However, much to his chagrin, she resisted his amorous advances. This may have had something to do with a physical disability she was afflicted with.

At the age of 11, when she was growing up in the Far East, a slavey of her brutal, unloving mother, she was knocked down by a lorry and her right foot so badly injured it had to be amputated. Although sharing a bed with Tambi she managed to conceal from him the fact that she wore a wooden foot. But there may have been another reason for her disinclination to allow him to 'have his way with her.'

At that time she was suffering, ironically enough, from unrequited love for Louis MacNeice. He had certainly been affected by the haunting quality of her appearance as demonstrated by the following lines from his poem *The Kingdom*:

> Too large in feature for a world of cuties,
> Too sculptured for a cocktail of cuties,
> This girl is almost awkward, carrying off
> The lintel of convention on her shoulders,
> Doric river-goddess with a pitcher
> Of ice-cold emotion. Pour them where she will
> The pitcher will not empty nor the steam grow warm
> But is so cold it burns . . .

Owing to lack of funds only one issue of *Poetry London* appeared that year. This was in November. Tony had been called up and Tambi sorely missed his practical abilities and steady drive. (I was shocked to see Tony, clad in khaki, clumping around in Army boots.) The Blitz had started in August. As I sat around with the Muttus one afternoon Tambi would gleefully exclaim from time to time: 'There's a German bomber overhead, you know.' As the weeks wore on, however, he found air raids less of a lark and when at home would hold a dustbin lid over his head during noisy periods. In contrast Jackie, calm and unflappable, declined to seek cover of any kind.

One afternoon Tambi and I went to the Apollo theatre to see *Thunder Rock*, a worthy but solemn anti-pacifist piece by Richard Ardey, in which Michael Redgrave played the lead. Towards the end of the first act air raids sirens brought the proceedings to an abrupt halt. 'Thank god, you know,' said Tambi. However, like most of the audience we did not leave the theatre to seek an air shelter. Redgrave had announced his intention of regaling those who stayed behind with a song or two. In the event he gave us three folk songs, which he delivered in a highly agreeable tenor voice. Then the all-clear sounded and it was back to *Thunder Rock*.

But the play appeared to have made a favourable impression on Tambi in the end. We were making our way up Shaftesbury Avenue when he suddenly declared: 'I'm going to join up, you know.' This announcement astonished me, for he was notoriously apolitical. I had never even heard him inveigh against British imperialism. I concluded he was entertaining a fantasy about the Great Muttu accomplishing glorious deeds on the battlefield. Then we passed a shabby, middle-aged man standing in the gutter. His chest was decorated with several war medals and he held a tray containing boxes of matches. The price, apparently, for one of those medals was the loss of his right leg. Tambi stared with dismay at the crutch on which he was leaning. I never heard him talk again of taking the King's shilling.

In time the Blitz began to wear the Muttus down and as a consequence they moved to Oxford, which was escaping the attention of the Luftwaffe. Before long, however, Tambi found himself craving Fitzrovia. Those dreaming spires afforded him scant compensation. Eventually they returned to the embattled capital.

About this time Jackie succeeded in breaking away from Tambi to from a relationship with Charles Hamblett, a poet and journalist. (In the fifties he published a biography of Humphrey Bogart.) He drank heavily, at which times he had an alarmingly wild aspect. Sadly, Jackie died some years later. She was diabetic, and substantiated rumour had it that she committed suicide by omitting to inject herself with insulin.

Tambi had found a basement flat in Oakley Gardens, Chelsea. At that time I was living not far away in Limerston Street. (I was then a full-time fire-watcher in the Fleet Street area.) I used to drop over every morning to cook a meal for both of us, Tambi being unable even to boil an egg. They were invariably Irish stews into which at the end of the cooking process I introduced several lumps of cheese. (Yielding to the spirit of the times I should perhaps have called these concoctions victory stews.)

One day I had just put the finishing touches to one of them when there was a knock on the front door. It turned out to be Kathleen Raine, the metaphysical poet. Lured into the kitchen by the odours emanating therefrom, she peered with curiosity into the pot containing the stew.

'Good heavens,' she exclaimed, 'I think I can see lumps of cheese in there.'

'Mature Canadian cheddar,' I informed her proudly.

'But you must never, absolutely never, put lumps of cheese into stews,' she declared in shocked tones.

Nevertheless, on the following day in went more lumps of cheese into the inevitable Irish stew. After all, I told myself defiantly, we were bohemians and supposed to do that sort of thing. Tambi had certainly made no complaints although, of course, he may well have thought that my Irish stews represented the original, unanglicized version.

As usual he was skulking in bed. I told him the meal was ready and he arose shakily to dress. As he sat glumly in front of the coal fire with his plate of stew in his lap I began to lecture him, somewhat priggishly, about his negative existence. No issue of the magazine had appeared for over a year. This was not altogether surprising since he divided his life more or less equally between boozing and sleeping.

Suddenly he stood up and hurled the plate and its contents into the fire. Ash-laden smoke filled the room. 'I can't stand your bloody damned platitudes, you know,' he shouted and stormed out of the flat.

Soon afterwards Tambi had a nervous breakdown. He took to his bed and turned his face to the wall. Left alone he might have starved to death but friends of his visited him and persuaded him to take sustenance. No persuasion was needed, however, where alcohol was concerned. T. S. Eliot helped him financially during his grim period.

But Tambi was soon on his feet again. *Poetry London* was resuscitated when Nicholson and Watson with his blessing took over the publishing side of the magazine. He now had a regular salary, for which he must have been grateful.

I encountered him one evening in the Swiss. Neither of us bothered to mention the incident of the flying plate of Irish stew. He complained about Sohoites who were always saying 'Dylan said . . .'. Mulk Raj Anand, the Indian novelist, joined us and began to rattle on about the essential differences between Eastern and Western ways of life. The speed of his delivery was truly amazing and rather comic. I tried to suppress a fit of giggles but failed. Tambi became similar afflicted. Mulk stopped, looked puzzled for a moment and then resumed his verbal barrage.

The Last Lamplighter

On another occasion Tambi and I were standing at the bar of the Bricklayers Arms when two GIs entered the pub. One of them ordered drinks while the other occupied himself with scowling at Tambi. He continued to scowl at him as he downed his whisky. Finally he addressed Tambi thus: 'What is a fucking nigger like you doing in here?' 'I'm a Tamil,' replied Tambi, 'and what is an ignorant lout like you doing here?' The soldier who had bought the drinks hastily interposed himself between Tambi and his buddy, whom he told to belt up. An ugly situation was thus rapidly refused.

'Last week, you know, a Yankee soldier attacked me outside the Mandrake Club,' Tambi said presently, 'I threw the fellow down the steps.' I did not doubt that it was true, for the Great Muttu in a rage was a force to be reckoned with.

One of our favourite haunts was the Caribbean Club, in Denman Street, whose members were a happy mixture of West Indians and Sohoites. The dark-skinned gentlemen tended to sport shiny, slicked-down hair and natty, gaberdine suits and move around the dance floor with nonchalant grace. Some of them were ponces who could usually be identified by their air of cool, lazy superiority. Odd musicians dropped in every evening to retail rhumbas, cha-chas, beguines and that sort of thing. Dennis Rose, the cadaverous bop trumpeter, turned up from time to time to blast our ears with dissonant harmonies. Calypso singers performed there sometimes. Rudi, the coloured owner of the club, who came from Martinique, seated himself importantly at the piano every night to sing 'J'Attendrai' with mawkish fervour. 'Oh my God, you know,' Tambi would mutter as if in pain. Brian Howard, the outrageous literary failure, occasionally put in an appearance. Sitting alone at a table, he exuded an air of distinguished melancholy. One night he said something to a young man who was standing near his table. The latter promptly smacked his face and walked angrily away. A fresh-faced George Melly, then still at Stowe, stormed into the club one evening with a gang of rowdy school mates. Having acquired drinks they launched into a lusty rendition of 'When The Saints Go Marching In'. Melly sang louder and more melodiously than the rest. This may well have been his first public performance in the West End.

Every night at the Fitzroy Arms Paul, a bearded homosexual in a kilt, knocked out popular tunes on an ancient upright. Tambi used to drop in to listen to him sometimes, for he loved this sort of music. He had published a few songs in Colombo before the war and once told me with a little giggle that you could then have bought in Woolworth's over here a record containing one of those immortal ditties.

Paul was also an artist. He once invited me to visit him to see some of his work. On entering his flat I was confronted by numerous sadistic drawings on his wall. They were of the most repellent nature imaginable. Suffice to say, uniformed Nazis figured in them prominently. I was glad to get out of the place.

There was another bearded homosexual sadist at large in Fitzrovia in those days. Possessed of a red face that twitched spasmodically, he was known as the Whipper of Ealing. He gave organ recitals in his local church where his audiences rarely consisted of more than a handful of people. Yet he played with flamboyant theatricality as if to an audience of thousands. 'I'm a Renaissance man,' he often declared in his high-pitched voice. He once visited Paul with fun and games in mind.

A problem arose, however, when they discovered that although both of them enjoyed inflicting pain neither of them liked to receive it. So they reluctantly took it in turns to be the passive partner.

Tambi moved into a large flat in Regent's Park Terrace whose owner had arranged for him to rent it while she was abroad. He offered me a rent-free room in exchange for cleaning the flat regularly and doing a spot of shopping from time to time. There was no mention of cooking meals. He now had lunch in restaurants. This was his sole meal of the day. I accepted his offer enthusiastically.

The arrangement did not work out terribly well. Shamefully, my cleaning efforts were cursory and infrequent. Tambi took me to task sometimes but only in the mildest of terms. My shopping forays were successful, or so it seemed to me. However, I overheard Tambi telling somebody in a pub one night that he thought I was fiddling the shopping bills. They were, in fact, scrupulously correct. It seems I was a victim of Tambi's paranoia. This could take the form of accusing a friend he had put up for the night of stealing his wallet, lost during the course of a pub crawl on the previous evening. More usually, however, it was waiters, taxi drivers and even bus conductors who aroused his irrational suspicions.

He could certainly be brutally frank at times. He once told Tony in his accordion playing days that he was all thumbs. One evening in the French he was drinking with an American when the latter confessed he had a low tolerance of alcohol. 'I can't stand a man who can't hold his liquor,' snapped Tambi. On another occasion he was talking in the same pub with a young man who had a tendency to blush frequently. 'Why are you always so red?', he demanded. 'Is it a disease or something?'

He was hopelessly childish, the result perhaps of being mollycoddles in his early years by numerous doting aunts.

Living in the moment as he did meant that his affairs were always in a mess. This led to frustration and misery. At those times he resembled a lost and bewildered child and it was impossible not to feel sorry for him. Nevertheless, in his happier moments, he displayed a captivating zest for life.

It could not be denied he had a kind and compassionate side. He once told me how distressed he used to be in his Colombo days to see in the fish market turtles lying helplessly on their back awaiting execution. When David Gascoyne suffered a mental breakdown he organized a fund for him. He liked to publish poems written by friends of his regardless of their merit, a highly reprehensible practice. I encountered him one night in the Swiss when I was suffering from a severe bout of unrequited love. To take the edge off my misery he persuaded me to stay in his flat for a few days.

Tambi did not have a regular girl friend, only the occasional bed-mate. One of these was a working-class girl, a 'mystery', who gave him a bad dose of the clap and, for good measure, nicked several *objets d'art*. A Hungarian lady graced his bed for a few nights. At that time he was proudly wearing a heavy belt that had encircled the massive girth of Roy Campbell, the South African poet, before he bequeathed it to Tambi during a drunken spree. One night Tambi removed the belt and, in a spirit of fun, chased her found the table in the sitting-room while whacking at her with the belt. 'This is Roy Campbell's belt, you know!' he cried: 'This is Roy Campbell's belt!' Then he clambered on to the table, folded his arms and shouted 'Make obeisance to the Great Muttu.'

David Gascoyne stayed one night in the spare bedroom. On the following morning he gleefully told us he had heard lions roaring in the night. He really had, for London Zoo, in Regent's Park, was only a quarter of a mile away.

The Last Lamplighter

Another friend of Tambi's, Harold Musson, stayed for several weeks. His father, a prosperous mine-owner, had died a year or so earlier and left him a small fortune. This enabled him to play the gad-about-Soho, which he did rather well thanks to his Oxford sophistication and infectious sense of fun. His girlfriend, who occasionally spent the night with him, used to flit about the flat topless much to Tambi's delight. However, Harold became drawn to Buddhism and before long became converted to the faith. He abandoned the flesh pots to go off to Ceylon and became a Buddhist monk. He shaved his head, assumed a saffron robe and adopted the title of the Venerable Nanvira Thera. For 16 years he lived alone in a bamboo hut in the jungle sustained only by food placed in his begging-bowl by Singhalese villagers. But he failed to find the spiritual bliss or whatever he was looking for and eventually committed suicide.

Gerald Wilde, the abstract expressionist painter, visited Tambi now and then. About this time he was doing some of his most compelling work, which had a lurid, nightmarish quality. He was alarmingly gaunt with intense, staring eyes. The shabby suit and wilted tie he invariably wore gave him an air of battered respectability. Generally broke, he used to badger customers in the French for small sums of money. Gaston would give him half-a-crown to go and drink in another pub but he would be back within an hour to claim another half-crown. He occasionally pawned his overcoat, redeemed it when he sold a painting and before long pawned it again. He was drinking in the French one wintry afternoon, having pawned his overcoat earlier, when a well-heeled acquaintance of his drifted in. Taking pity on Gerald he slipped out of the expensive tweed overcoat and gave it to him. Some hours later Gerald sold it to somebody in the pub for the price of a few drinks. 'Look at all those vacant faces,' he exclaimed as we were walking down Oxford Street one morning, 'Hundreds and hundreds of grey blobs. How I loathe them!'

Tambi, Gerald and myself were gloomily sitting around one Sunday afternoon in Tambi's flat when Gerald suddenly rose to his feet, strode to the door, locked it and put the key in his pocket. 'We've all had enough, I think, of this hell known as living,' he declared. Whereupon he went over to the gas fire – it had no pilot light – and turned it on deliberately omitting to light it. Gas fumes poured into the room. 'Gerald, old boy, don't be silly, you know,' said Tambi and reached over to turn off the gas tap.

As well as bringing out issues of the magazine Tambi was publishing books under the imprint of *Editions Poetry London*. Among them were *The Cosmological Eye* by Henry Miller, *The Real Life of Sebastian Knight* by Vladimir Nabokov, *Under a Glass Bell* by Anais Nin and *By Grand Central Station I Sat Down and Wept* by Elizabeth Smart.

However, profits failed to materialize. Nicholson and Watson eventually threw in the towel. They were succeeded by Richard March, a teacher of languages among many other things. But the board of directors decided before long that Tambi's disorderly working habits were a liability they could ill afford. As a result he was forced to resign from the firm.

During the war Tony Dickins had attained the rank of major. When it was all over he returned to his old bohemian haunts but now found them distasteful. Heavy drinking has always been an important part of Soho life but it was an occupation that had little appeal for Tony. The rumbustious, anti-social behaviour that often accompanied it was also unappealing to him. So he gave up Soho and in future was wont to refer to its inhabitants as a crowd of hooligans.

He found a teaching job at the City of London Literary

The Last Lamplighter

Institute and later published several books on chess. He visited Wormwood Scrubbs Prison regularly to play chess with lifers. He was a brilliant amateur pianist and gave an occasional recital in a church.

He died of cancer in his early seventies.

In 1949 Tambi returned to Ceylon and later visited India where he met Safia whom, shortly afterwards, he married. In the early 50s they emigrated to the States and settled down in New York. He brought out four issues of what had now become *Poetry London/New York* and wrote some short stories that were published here and there. The couple experienced much poverty that was partly due to Tambi's heavy drinking. It became clear to him that he could not offer Safia a reasonable life and he persuaded her to return to Ceylon. Before long, however, he married for the third time. She was an American woman, called Esta, who bore him a daughter. In the late 60s he returned to London in order to make a fresh start in the publishing world. Esta elected to remain behind with their daughter.

I received a shock when Tambi walked into the French one night. When I had last seen him 20 years earlier he was young and exceedingly handsome. I now beheld an emaciated old man with lifeless eyes. His grey hair, though, was still plentiful. He wore a dark blue Indian tunic. He greeted me without smiling and said that it was strange seeing me with grey hair. Nevertheless he said he was glad to be back in England, where, in contrast to the States, people did things for other people without wanting anything in return.

His return to this country did not go unnoticed by the press. There were articles about him, interviews and photographs in various newspapers and magazines. He put on weight and began to look like a living member of the human race again. However, his life was in the usual hopeless mess due to financial extravagance. Ill health, moreover, now dogged him and he was prey to frequent bouts of deep depression.

In spite of all this he travelled to India in the early '80s in order to meet Mrs Gandhi, then Prime Minister of India, and discuss with her his idea of an Indian Arts Council based in London. It seems that the notion appealed to her strongly and Tambi returned to England in a sanguine mood.

At that time he was living in a flat above the October Gallery in Great Ormond Street. To reach the flat he had to ascend an iron staircase outside the building. As he was climbing the staircase one evening he suddenly tripped and fell. The two American ladies who owned the gallery heard the noise and found him lying unconscious at the bottom of the staircase. An ambulance was summoned immediately.

As he lay in his hospital bed Tambi knew that his injuries were severe and that he did not have long to live – in fact it was only a few days. Even at this late hour, however, he did not abandon his cherished project. From his hospital bed he dictated letters to Jane Williams, his secretary and friend, in which he solicited financial aid from well-heeled acquaintances of his with cultural interests. Shortly after his death Jane received a telegram of condolence from Mrs Gandhi.

After the funeral service, which ended with a Welsh harpist playing a melancholy air of his native country, I made my way to the October Gallery where a wake was in progress. I met there Tambi's teenage daughter, Shakentala, who physically resembled an Indian girl but, bold, self-confident and forthright, was entirely American in spirit. Sir John Waller, an old friend of Tambi, sat by himself sipping wine and looking sombre. He was then living in Brighton and composing limericks for *Gay News*. Eddie Linden, the

The Last Lamplighter

Scottish poet and editor of *Aquarius*, became very drunk and declaimed poems at his captive audience. I fell into conversation with Claire MacAlister, the American poetess, who had known Tambi in his New York days. She was an attractive, middle-aged woman with red hair and wore quietly elegant clothes. One of her favourite memories of Tambi she told me, was of his meeting her father, a high-ranking judge, who had invited them to dine with him in a posh restaurant. Tambi was often unkempt and ill-dressed but on this occasion he turned up wearing a well-laundered Indian tunic and spotlessly clean trousers with a knife-edge crease. Above all he had the well-scrubbed look of a child about to take communion.

Our conversation was interrupted by an unexpected announcement from one of the owners of the gallery to the effect that a belly dancing class was due to start in half-an-hour. She apologized for having to ask us to vacate the room. In my imagination I heard Tambi chuckling at this bizarre end to his wake.

Years later Tony Dickins unveiled in the foyer of the Purcell Room a bronze bust of Tambi executed by a contemporary Sri Lankan sculptor. The ceremony preceded a concert in the Purcell Room that had been organized by the Bloomsbury Ceylonese Group. The concert consisted of music-making, dancing and poetry readings, the participants mainly Sri Lankan. For some reason a group of Scottish dancers clad in tartan took over for a couple of numbers but their lively cavortings, though inappropriate, were highly enjoyable.

However, before the show, Tony, as he stood before the bust which was covered by a dark cloth, had given an address to members of the Bloomsbury Ceylonese Group, in which he summarized Tambi's life and achievements. Then he removed the cloth from the bust and as he did so my heart sank, for I beheld a romantic, idealized portrayal of Tambi, the only merit of which was a vague physical resemblance to the poet as a young man. An elderly gentleman, probably a member of the group, who was standing on the other side of the bust, took the cloth from Tony and handed him a crown of palm leaves. This Tony solemnly placed on the bust but, owing to bad eyesight, at a comically rakish angle. The elderly gentleman hastily re-adjusted it. Again I heard those celestial chuckles from Tambi.

Jackie

I first met Jackie in the early 50s in the Lyons Corner House in Coventry Street. It was around midnight – an hour when the restaurant wore a louche air that contrasted markedly with the genteel atmosphere prevailing earlier, and most apparent in the afternoon when a piano trio performed light music in a studiously polite manner. Later in the evening office clerks and shop assistants were replaced by professional gamblers, jazz musicians and their girl friends, Sohoites, villains and street walkers taking the weight off their feet for half-an-hour.

Jackie was sitting at a table with a couple of jazz musicians whom I knew slightly. She was sipping black coffee and smoking furiously. She had slightly aquiline features, fair hair and compelling blue eyes. Her voice bore traces of an accent that would have been either Irish or Northern American. She was attired in the elegant style of the 50s when tight-waisted outfits and long skirts were *de rigueur*. All I can remember of the conversation was that she said she wanted to learn to play the piano. She was 23 and full of hope.

One of my Soho haunts in those days was Happy Blake's,

Jackie

a West Indian dive in Kingley Street. Few Sohoites found their way to the club since it was situated on the remote western fringes of the village. Bob Wardlaw, a genial bewhiskered Scot and a friend of mine, used to pound the ivories down there night after night in the manner of Fats Waller, though without his vocal interjections. Bob had recently toured the country with Shirley Bassey, then a blues singer, as her accompanist. Fledgling jazz musicians, usually sax players, turned up sometimes at Happy Blake's to jam with Bob.

One evening I dropped into the club and, somewhat to my surprise, found Jackie working down there as a waitress. I had not seen her since our first meeting some weeks earlier. She greeted me warmly and I was again aware of her compelling blue eyes.

The club, as usual, closed at midnight. Having decided that it was 'Ovaltine time' for him, Bob disappeared and Jackie and I betook ourselves to a café nearby. As we chatted over coffees I was aware of a powerful mutual attraction. It seemed almost inevitable that we spent the night together and Jackie came home with me.

As we lay in bed that night Jackie talked at great length about her past life. She had been born in Rosslea, County Fermanagh, in Northern Ireland. Her father, John Creighan, had worked as an engineer for a local Ford factory. Her mother, Mary, was the daughter of a peasant farmer. In his bachelor days John had been a notorious philanderer. Nevertheless the wedding had not been a shot gun affair. For whatever reason, however, he fled to the States 13 months after the event leaving Mary with a 3-month-old baby, who had been christened Maureen.

Two or three weeks later Mary received a small sum of money from her absent spouse which was the sole extent of the financial aid she ever got from him. For a time she was actually starving and unable to feed her baby. She also faced the imminent prospect of eviction from her home. In desperation she sought help from her parents who took them both in.

However, Mary needed money and jobs were scarce in Northern Ireland at that time. She decided that she would eventually have to go to England in search of employment. She waited until Maureen was three years old and then departed for England. This was a heart-breaking experience for Mary. A sister of hers put her up for a while in her Ealing flat. Before long, however, Mary found a job as a home help to a rich old lady who lived in a house in Kensington. Similar jobs followed, which enabled her to move into an unfurnished flat in a mews – a real one with horses and stables – in the Royal Borough. Every week she sent a portion of her wages to her parents and later had Maureen educated at some expense at a private Catholic school in Rosslea.

Mary spent her summer holidays and Christmas breaks at the farm. Maureen looked forward to her visits in a state of feverish excitement and found her departures heart-rending. Mary suffered equally.

Maureen was mainly brought up by two unmarried aunts, who also lived on the farm. They were kindly and well-intentioned but a bit rough and ready compared to her mother, a gentle, soft-spoken, innately refined woman. She would certainly not have given Maureen sandwiches wrapped in sheets of old newspapers to take to school in the morning as they were wont to do. As a consequence Maureen would seek a secluded spot at lunchtime and there, unobserved by other girls, delve into her satchel for her midday snack and its shameful wrappers.

She often thought about her father who had settled down

Jackie

in New York. Having persuaded her mother to give her his address she wrote to him and eagerly awaited a reply. None came however.

Mary had decided that she should leave the farm when her schooldays ended and come to live with her in London. The day duly arrived and Maureen departed for the capital in a state of almost uncontrollable excitement. She was met at Liverpool Station by her mother, who was accompanied by a strange man. Mary introduced them to each other and she learned that his name was Dick Dimbleby. Maureen had always imagined that her mother would whisk her away to the mews in a taxi on this very special day. However, Dick said that they should travel by bus and Mary deferred to his decision. Maureen thought that it was none of his business and wondered why he was going home with them.

Over cups of tea in the flat Mary, a simple Catholic woman, brought herself with great difficulty to confess to Maureen that she had been living with Dick for several years. She had wanted to get a divorce from John but he had declined to answer any of her letters. Maureen, then a naïve Catholic girl, was deeply shocked by her mother's confession. She suffered a further shock when she learnt that she would not be staying at the flat after all but would be dumped on Dick's mother, who lived alone in a house in Chiswick. One can only assume that Mary felt so guilt-ridden over her relationship with Dick that she could not bear the thought of her young daughter living in these sinful surroundings.

Dick, an engineer, was a bluff, genial, decent man, who was deeply devoted to Mary. Eschewing pubs and race meetings he liked nothing better than sitting around in the flat reading newspapers and listening to the radio.

Before long Maureen found a job as a typist at a branch

of Lloyds in the City, which must have gratified Mary. But Maureen hated the job and loathed the City. Her sole consolation in those bleak days were visiting her mother, which she did frequently.

The house in Chiswick was ugly and bleak with a pervasive smell of must and wax polish. Maureen had little in common with Mrs Dimbleby and dreaded having to share a meal with her and struggle to make conversation. During one of the meals Mrs Dimbledy confided to her with pride that she always added a few soda crystals to the water in which she was boiling green cabbage leaves in order to make them greener. At night in bed – this was in 1944 – Maureen would hear the occasional drone of a doodle bug and tremble.

One day she decided that she had had enough of this drab existence. She chucked her job in the bank to work as a hostess in a night club in Marylebone and escaped from the house in Chiswick to move into a small flat near the club. She also began to haunt bop clubs. By then she had ceased to be Maureen and become Jackie.

At that time bop was a revolutionary kind of jazz music characterized by dissonant chords and jagged cross rhythms, two of its chief practitioners being Charlie Parker and Dizzy Gillespie. Eleven British bop musicians, Ronnie Scott among them, founded a club in Great Windmill Street and called it Club Eleven. They used a rehearsal room whose sole source of illumination was a single naked bulb hanging from the ceiling. There were no seats for the members of the club who stood around imbibing the music or indulging in a spot of token dancing on the limited floor space. Jackie visited the club frequently and got to know the musicians and their girl friends, who also haunted Harmony Inn. This was an unpretentious café just around the corner from Club Eleven and opposite the headquarters of the Musicians Union. The

Jackie

café was dominated by a football table which Ronnie Scott played obsessively. Most members of this circle smoked pot and a few dabbled in hard drugs.

A colourful character in the bop world was Peggy Robinson, otherwise known as Bopping Peggy. A small attractive redhead she had a huge sense of fun and a seemingly unlimited capacity for living it up. Her parting words to friends were almost invariably 'Keep raving, folks!' At bop clubs she used to dance with captivating sinuosity, and was always the last member to leave. She had a posh voice but liked to employ the jargon of the jazz world. Thus she might say 'Let's dig the scene at Wizard's, man', or 'That cat plays a real cool horn', but always in that posh accent. She had a big generous heart and a trusting nature that made her an easy prey for sharks.

The sole mourner at the cremation of an alcoholic friend of hers, who had died of cirrhosis of the liver, Peggy left the crematorium bearing a casket containing the ashes of her friend. In the early hours of the following morning she buried the casket under an elm tree facing a pub her friend used to frequent. About this time she took on a job as the manageress of a club in Knightsbridge. She got plastered one night – the owner was away at the time – and invited members of the club to help themselves to drinks behind the bar. When the owner heard of this escapade he sent her packing. She was married for a few years to Ken Wray, a high-ranking bop trombonist. After their divorce she used to refer to herself as Peggy X-Ray.

Jackie had an affair with a Jewish boy whom she loved for his romantic, poetic nature. She became pregnant and had an abortion after which their relationship petered out. Many years later she read with incredulity a report in a daily newspaper of a court case in which her erstwhile boy friend had been charged with organizing a prostitution ring and bribing the police to turn a blind eye to his activities.

Her next boy friend was Lucky, an ostentatiously nonchalant Nigerian who was studying art at the Central. They sometimes visited the Roebuck, a pub mainly inhabited by West Indians, which stood on the corner of Maple Street and Tottenham Court Road. (It is now a comfortable, tastefully furnished establishment called Flintlock and Pitcher). The main purpose of their visits was to buy hashish from one of the numerous drug dealers that plied their trade in the bar. Their mission accomplished, they would leave the pub to cross the road and plunge into the Paramount Dance Hall. (This is now The Cockney where cabaret is performed nightly). It was populated in the main by West Indians and young women with complexions in various shades of black and white. Here and there the acrid smell of pot hung in the air. A 15 piece band composed of bop musicians belted out jazz standards. The police raided the hall from time to time and were not averse to planting hemp on customers.

Although the drug usually has a soothing effect on its imbibers Jackie and Lucky had a furious row one night in the Paramount, and at closing time she refused to leave with him. He responded by crooking a forefinger round a necklace she was wearing and leading her out into the street and down to Warren Street Station. By then she had calmed down somewhat and they made it up.

Lucky was eventually succeeded by Dizzy, who was also a Nigerian. Although good-looking he lacked his predecessors charm and personality and Jackie soon tired of him. As they were sitting in her flat one evening she told him that she wanted to end the affair. Dizzy reacted by whipping out a knife and savagely attacking the contents of her wardrobe. Then he stormed out of the flat. Enraged by his behaviour

Jackie

Jackie rang up the police. There was a court case and Dizzy spent several weeks in prison.

Thus ended Jackie's nocturnal account of her life so far. One thing, however, puzzled me and I asked her why she had given up her job hostessing to work as a waitress at Happy Blake's where she could not have earned much money. She said she found the job less disagreeable than making conversation with drunken lecherous business men in the middle of the night.

At that time I was living in an unfurnished room in a house in Delamere Terrace in Paddington. The terrace consisted of crumbling Victorian houses overlooking the Grand Union Canal. My room was on the second floor but it was the room next to mine, occupied by Hal Woolf, a middle-aged painter, that had the view. Jackie moved in a week or so after our first night together. It was a surprising thing for her to have done in view of the determinedly bohemian character of the room and the conspicuous lack of creature comforts.

In my mind's eye I see a Primus stove standing in the middle of the room whose uncarpeted floor is strewn with discarded newspapers and magazines. An upended orange box contains books, two enamelled mugs and a packet of biscuits. On a refectory table lies a variety of objects that include a copper plated trumpet, an Arban trumpet, sheets of popular music, more books, numerous 10" wax records, and a pair of bicycle clips. Here and there stands an empty quart-sized beer bottle (Each of them is worth tuppence when returned to the local off license). Taped to a wall is a photograph of Greta Garbo torn from a magazine. A light bulb draped in a red cotton scarf hangs from the ceiling and bathes the room at night in a crimson glow.

We shared with Hal a tiny kitchen that was next to the laboratory on the landing below. There was no bathroom.

The Last Lamplighter

Jackie would bathe at her mother's while Hal and I would use the Porchester Public Baths in Porchester Road. For a shilling you had a cubicle and a bath half-filled with warm water, a thin bath towel and a tablet of cheap yellow soap. The bath taps were connected to pipes outside the cubicle and if, therefore, you wanted a top up you had to summon the attendant by dint of bawling out the number of your cubicle.

In those days I was working as a lamplighter and learning to play the trumpet. (A friend of mine once referred disparagingly to my instrument as Fothergill's folly).

Jackie was warm-hearted, fun-loving, quarrelsome, pig-headed and violent. She was not in the least wifely. She did not relentlessly ply me with food, for instance, or ever urge me to wrap up before issuing forth on a wintry night. She was acutely aware of the less admirable aspects of my character, which were numerous and which she attacked mercilessly. This, of course, did me a power of good. However, she was also absurdly jealous. On one occasion she accused me of flirting with the stout middle-aged Cockney lady who lived on the top floor of the house. When I contemptuously dismissed the charge she suddenly grabbed an empty pint-sized milk bottle and brought it down on my head.

Relating a story to Jackie was always an uphill struggle since she would continually interrupt the flow with questions about various details. At these times, indeed, she had the manner of a hostile detective interrogating the witness of a serious crime. This could be irritating but even more so was her behaviour at a cinema where, as we sat watching a feature film, she would frequently ask me to repeat a scrap of dialogue she had missed. I did so dutifully but these verbal exchanges meant that I could never relax and get lost in a movie. One night these interruptions exasperated me so much that I transferred myself to another part of the cinema. We walked home in silence and then had a first-class row during which I acquired a black eye.

She was woefully ignorant despite her expensive education. By way of an example, we were having a fierce argument about Irish affairs one day when it became apparent that she thought that Ireland was still part of the United Kingdom. She possessed two books, Hemingway's *The Sun also Rises* and Graham Greene's *The End of the Affair*, which, having read, she returned to again and again. She would dash off drawings in a sketch book that were strong and decisive and showed promise. Having attended a few art classes at St Martin's, however, she dropped out, intimidated, apparently, by the superior skill of her fellow students.

Shortly after moving in Jackie gave up her job at Happy Blake's and so we used to spend the evening drinking red wine, talking, listening to music – she was not too keen on the classical stuff – and making love. Before long, however, we both began to miss Soho, Jackie's Soho being bop clubs and Harmony Inn, and mine various bohemian bars, clubs and cafés. So we gradually drifted back to our old haunts. Jackie would usually issue forth in the afternoon, thereby allowing me to feel free to practice my trumpet.

Hal, of course, was very much part of our lives in those days. Then in his fifties he had haggard good looks, pale blue mistrustful eyes and grey wavy hair that resembled corrugated iron. He had an endearing habit of uttering a tiny yelp of pleasure whenever he heard something that was piquant and amusing. He had a malevolent-looking cat called Beauty to whom he was inexplicably devoted. His untidy, cluttered room, which overlooked the canal, was dominated by a mural that consisted of a mass of ghostly sinister faces.

Hal had been a highly successful portrait painter in the

The Last Lamplighter

30s with a studio in Chelsea. Towards the end of the decade he married Greta, a boisterous German with short fair hair, bright blue eyes and a snub nose. Her sturdy, shapely legs had fascinated Frank Dobson the English sculptor, for whom she modeled on several occasions. The Army claimed Hal in 1940 and he spent most of the war in Cairo as a camouflage artist. He rose in time to the rank of captain. The long separation endured by Hal and Greta eventually destroyed their marriage but they remained good friends.

Back in civvies Hal picked up the threads of his pre-war career. As before, however, his sitters invariably expressed dissatisfaction with the finished product. They all wanted to possess a flattering image of themselves but this Hal declined to provide. He stuck it for a couple of years and then, sick of the whole business, chucked it in.

Thereafter he subsisted on a succession of jobs that could be described as menial. He was a van driver for a time and then a public lamplighter, after which he worked in a Wall's ice cream factory and then a paint factory. From the last mentioned he used to smuggle out bottles of pure methylated spirit and at home lace glasses of orange juice with the potent liquid.

On Sunday mornings, provided the weather was reasonably good, he would set out with an easel and painting materials to paint local scenes. These included a stretch of the canal, the Victorian church at the end of the terrace and a bombed site overgrown with flowers, weeds and bushes. Sadly however, his efforts, although well-crafted, lacked verve and sparkle. He came to realize this in time and eventually gave up the struggle. Henceforth, he decided, he would live for the weekends, when, liberated temporarily from drudgery, he would seek to create an artificial paradise by means of alcohol, marihuana and benzedrine.

Jackie

On Friday evenings Hal would smoke a joint, drink two or three glasses of wine, and visit a theatre or cinema. If he stayed at home he would listen to the radio. He was religiously devoted to Radio 3 and the Home Service, stations which in those days had extremely high standards. On Saturday mornings he drifted down to the French pub where he met Greta and a few old cronies. Later he went off in search of the drug dealer from whom he bought his weekly supply of 'West African weed'. Having returned home he prepared his room for the evening party. (Hal and Jackie and I threw open our doors to all and sundry on Saturday evenings). Connie, Hal's Cockney girl friend, would spend the night with him and on the following morning set out groggily for Marylebone where she worked in a pub as a barmaid. Hal would wander over to the Warwick Castle on the other side of the canal. He felt agreeably relaxed in this middle-class pub with its quiet, sedate atmosphere that was in such marked contrast to the noisy jollifications of the previous night. The customers prized Hal as a charming eccentric and Hal, for his part, was more than happy to hold forth for an hour or so to an appreciative audience. At closing time – it was two o'clock on the Sabbath in those days – he would make his way back to his room and there revive his flagging energies with the aid of a benzedrine inhaler. He then dropped in on Bo and Ruby Milton, theatre folk, and their three young daughters who all lived on the first floor. The children on whom Hal bestowed little presents from time to time regarded him as a kind of benign, doting uncle. Revved up on benzedrine, however, Hal talked at the family rather than with them. When his monologizing began to run out of steam he would leave his bemused audience and repair to his kitchen. Sipping wine the while, he would carefully prepare a special meal and then consume it slowly and

The Last Lamplighter

appreciatively. Having cleared up he would retire to his room. The rest of the evening he spent stretched out on his bed listening to the radio, bestirring himself only to switch from Radio 3 to the Home Service. Sometimes he fell asleep with his radio on. When I heard a steady, persistent whine in the early hours of the morning I would creep into his room and turn off his set.

Our Saturday night parties were an institution in the 50s. People, mostly Sohoites, would turn up on impulse in the certainty of finding a party in progress. If Hal was away on holiday Jackie and I would hold the fort and vice versa. Hal had a collection of party records, mainly HMV 78s with mauve labels that consisted of pre-war recordings by Cuban bands of rhumbas and beguines. They were his pride and joy. He would sometimes clonk away on a pair of claves as his gramophone played one of these records. Sadly, however, he failed to master any of the required rhythmic patterns, which caused him considerable frustration. His face contorted by a violent effort of concentration, he would try to work them out mathematically but to no avail.

As Jackie and I lay in bed at night we would hear Hal and Connie having a prolonged, noisy row. One night, however, Jackie and I were drifting off to sleep after one of these benzedrine-induced brawls when somebody rapped on our door in a highly peremptory manner. I opened it to find myself confronted by Hal, who was white with anger. He told me that he had just found the smouldering remains of food in three blackened saucepans on the gas stove. He accused me of ruining these saucepans which we shared. I pointed out to him that it was he, not Jackie or myself, who had left food cooking on the stove and forgotten all about it.

Three Nigerian musicians, friends of Hal, would often

turn up on Saturday nights. A professional group, two of them guitarists and the other a bongo player, they performed music of their native land. At the parties they would sit around listening intently to the Cuban records, drawing on shared reefers and chuckling appreciatively at the felicities of the music. One evening they brought along their instruments and let rip, which was a joyous and exhilarating experience.

Understandably, however, neighbours became exceedingly restive when the singing, strumming and banging went on until well after midnight. Having learnt that guests were being attacked as they left the house, Hal, Jackie and I tore down the stairs to the street where I was immediately set upon by a lorry driver who lived next door. He knocked me to the ground and began swishing at me with a bicycle chain. Fortunately his aim was poor and I received no facial injuries. I managed to struggle to my feet whereupon he set about strangling me. He might well have succeeded had not a police van arrived in the nick of time. For several days I was unable to speak above a hoarse whisper and black marks adorned my neck for weeks. Jackie emerged from the fray with severe bruising. Hal, owing perhaps to his gray locks, came out of it unscathed. The Nigerians had prudently remained indoors during these unpleasant happenings but later found that the tyres of their car had been slashed.

One afternoon I came home from work to find Jackie lying on the bed staring at the ceiling with glazed eyes. She seemed to be unaware of my presence. Later she sat up and began to talk in a silly, giggly sort of way that irritated me. I had to go back to my job but when I returned I found her wandering about the room babbling incoherently. Ruby was sitting on a chair near the door and watching her anxiously. She told me that Hal wanted to see me. He was talking to

The Last Lamplighter

Bo in his room and they both looked exceedingly grave. Hal told me that, an hour or so earlier, Jackie had walked out of the house completely naked and visited a married couple, acquaintances of hers, who lived a few doors away. The wife had thrown an overcoat over her and led her back to the house. Hal said he thought that she was in urgent need of hospital treatment. Bo concurred. In a somewhat dazed condition I made my way to the telephone kiosk nearby and dialed the emergency number. As Jackie sat in the ambulance between two ambulance men she waved at me gaily as if she were going off on holiday. The driver closed the doors, returned to his seat and the ambulance departed.

She was taken to Bansted Hospital where she stayed for several weeks and received insulin treatment. On Sunday afternoons Mary, Dick and myself visited the hospital where we found her withdrawn and uncommunicative. After her discharge she remained in this condition for two or three weeks and then made a recovery of sorts. Months later, however, she suffered a relapse and had to be readmitted to the hospital. This time she underwent electro-convulsive therapy. In those days patients were not given a general anaesthetic before the administration of the electric shock, which caused a momentary epileptic fit. Jackie would lie on her bed in the ward awaiting her turn as the doctor with his terrifying equipment worked his way from bed to bed. This draconian treatment, however, did not prevent her from having another mental collapse after her discharge. This time I kept her at home and nursed her through it, though at the expense of many sleepless nights. While staying with her mother, as she did occasionally by now, she had yet another breakdown but her mother followed my example and got her through it.

I never seemed to survive a week in these days without

Jackie

having to pay a visit to the local pawnbroker. Like all pawnbrokers in poor districts at that time he accepted a huge variety of articles that included clocks, cutlery, blankets and clothes, almost anything indeed provided it was in good condition. Towards the end of the week I would visit 'uncle' with a sports jacket, perhaps, or an overcoat – I resolutely declined ever to pawn my trumpet – and redeemed it on Saturday. So I listened with keen interest one day to a friend of mine, who was aware of my financial problems, when he suggested that I marry Jackie in order to claim the tax rebate. As I was opposed to the institution of marriage I should have rejected the idea out of hand. However, I consulted Jackie on the subject and she agreed. I had, at least, been entirely honest about my reason for wanting to legalize our relationship, which in any case I considered a lasting one.

We were married at Paddington Registrar Office in Harrow Road. Mary, of course, attended the ceremony but, doubtless regretting her daughter's choice of husband, looked far from happy. It was either Hal or Bo – it is strange that I am hazy about this – who acted as the best man. Jackie had donned for the occasion a pale green beret, which I had never seen before. She must have worn it years ago in Ireland. She had seemed serenely unaware of its incongruity as, arm in arm, we walked up the stairs of the registrar office. All of a sudden I felt a surge of pity for the bride to be.

I found myself deeply resenting the ceremony. The relationship between Jackie and myself was being institutionalised and I did not like it a bit. During the proceedings, moreover, the registrar wore an expression I can only describe as lascivious. When I slipped the ring on her finger he formed an o with his mouth and drew in his breath sharply. After the ghastly business was over Mary bestowed on him a pound note.

The Last Lamplighter

Some weeks later Jackie and I were sitting around at home chatting when she began to fumble in her handbag for a packet of cigarettes. Suddenly a hypodermic fell out. She offered no explanation. I could only conclude that she was injecting herself with heroin. I was stunned for a moment. Then a feeling of utter revulsion overwhelmed me. I lost control and hit her, an action for which I have always felt ashamed.

It seemed that she had been dabbling in heroin for several months. It started when one of her girl friends persuaded her to give it a whirl and had even, owing to Jackie's squeamishness, given her the injection herself. These revelations shocked me and I begged her to give up her drug taking, which I imagined could only be a temporary aberration.

During the following weeks I sometimes felt that she had given herself a fix but she always denied it. Knowing her to be an unusually honest person I believed her. Nevertheless, suspicions nagged at me. This uncertainty was one of the worst aspects of the situation. One day I felt absolutely convinced that she was stoned despite her protestations to the contrary. Suddenly I grabbed her handbag, opened it and found among its contents a hypodermic needle. In a fit of impotent rage I hurled it to the floor and stamped on it.

Like all people who begin to dabble in hard drugs she suffered from the delusion that she would take them or leave them. By now, however, she had become an addict and acknowledged the fact. She decided to take a cure and was eventually admitted to Maudsley Hospital. In common with most hospitals it had by now abandoned the cold turkey treatment for drug addicts. This had consisted simply of withholding the drug from patients, thereby subjecting them to three or four days of physical and emotional torment. Instead, patients were now given medicine to offset withdrawal symptoms.

Jackie

While Jackie was in hospital I called one evening on Laura, a drug-addicted friend of hers, who lived in the neighbourhood. She was remarkably slender with slightly oriental features and always elegantly attired. She did secretarial work of some kind or other. As we sat around talking in her bed-sitter her record player retailed a recording of a stoned Billy Holliday wearily performing mournful ballads. Laura said that she was amazed that I had never taken heroin. I imagined that she was still in the honeymoon period of heroin addiction and had yet to reach the joyless stage when an addict only had a fix in order to fend off withdrawal symptoms. I told her I would never have any truck with a drug that caused so much human misery and was so powerfully addictive. I also said that I regarded the use of a hypodermic needle as an obscenity. I expressed as well a deep loathing of the emotionally deadening effect of heroin on its users.

Presently, out of the blue, Laura made a somewhat startling proposition. She said that if I gave her a pound every week I could have as much sex with her as I liked. I declined the offer mainly because I was not prepared to be unfaithful to Jackie. I never told her about Laura's proposition and in time, for one reason or another, she dropped out of our lives. One day, however, I found myself sitting next to her on a double decker. I was shocked by her shabby appearance about which she seemed blithely unconcerned. This was the last time I ever saw her. Months later she died of an overdose of heroin.

Jackie returned home after her cure but it seemed she was unable to stay off the drug. She eventually had another cure and yet another, both of them with a similar dismal result. Nevertheless, I continued to hope that she would ultimately give it up.

The Last Lamplighter

In those days heroin addicts could legally obtain a prescription for the drug from GPs. Once established, however, the dosage remained the same. But the drug only had the desired effect if the dosage was continually increased. This meant that addicts had to buy from drug dealers the extra supplies they needed. So Jackie, unbeknownst to me, was also topping up her prescribed dose in this manner. (Despite my vigorous opposition to the idea, she had gone back to hostessing). When she found that she was having to fork out large sums of money to drug pushers she took a cure and then started again from scratch. Thus these cures were not genuine ones.

When I learnt from one of her friends of this deception I was shocked and angry. I now realised that I had been playing second fiddle to her drug addiction all this time. Henceforth we led separate lives, though continuing to dwell under the same roof. This was possible since, at the time of the break up, we were inhabiting a flat in Porchester Square which had five rooms.

I now see that Jackie, in view of her mental condition, could hardly be blamed for her drug taking. And drug addicts, like alcoholics, do tend to lie about their habit. Jackie mentioned, moreover, that heroin was the only drug that could still the hyperactivity from which she suffered from time to time and which she described as a kind of emotional seething. She insisted that this condition had nothing to do with sexual frustration. Perhaps I should have shown more understanding but I developed a moralistic attitude and hatred of the junkie scene.

Towards the end of her life Jackie became a semi-invalid as a result of a stroke and the onset of emphysema, caused by her excessive devotion to small cigars. We were then living in a small council house in East Acton. One day she

Jackie

had a bad fall and fractured a hip. The hip replacement operation was successful but she contracted pneumonia and died as a consequence. She was 58.

Some Soho Characters

*QUENTIN CRISP, JIMMY THE BAKER, SIGNOR FAVA,
DAVID ARCHER, W. S. GRAHAM, CANADIAN RAY,
REDVERS GRAY, BRYCE MACNABB,
THE ROBERTS ET AL*

Gaston Berlemont succeeded his father, Victor, as landlord of the York Minster, known to its habitués as the French, in 1949. Like his father he had kindly eyes and a handlebar moustache. A robustly extrovert manner concealed innate shyness. He liked to tell hearty jokes and do tricks with an old piece of string. When a woman entered the pub who was not a 'regular' he was liable to greet her in a stagey French accent and kiss the back of her hand along which he sometimes ran his famous moustache. The latter action elicited muffled shrieks of protest from the more timorous of his victims.

If he became aware of anyone creating a scene he would bear down on the offender and calmly enquire if he, or she, were all right. This usually did the trick, for Gaston had a formidable presence. In his younger days he had to content with much unrest in his pub. Fisticuffs and face-slapping were then the order of the day. Paul Potts had a habit of kicking people in the shins when they offended him. Being a woman afforded no immunity from these assaults. 'Regulars' as well were wont to fling the contents of their glass into the face of somebody they disliked. If their aim was poor, as it often was owing to their advanced state of intoxication, an innocent bystander could suffer.

Gaston was loth to bar any of his customers. One night, however, he imposed the Supreme Penalty on a drunken journalist who, incensed by his refusal to serve him, had thrown a clumsy punch that landed on his shoulder. Another boozy journalist suffered the same fate. Prone to bombarding all and sundry in the pub with crude insults, he unwisely disregarded Gaston's stern reprimands. One day he called Gaston a Belgian cunt. 'Out' thundered Gaston, 'and don't dare to show your nasty face in here again.' (His father had been born in France near the border with Belgium, hence the mistaken notion that he was Belgian.) Gaston was once invited by an incorrigible troublemaker he had just barred to step outside. 'By all means, sir', said Gaston cheerfully. Once outside, however, his potential sparring partner made a lame excuse and sloped off. On one notable occasion Gaston sacked a member of his staff and barred her at the same time. An attractive young lady with a posh accent, she had drunk like a trooper behind the bar and hurled foul oaths at customers. 'Besides', Gaston told me later, 'I couldn't afford her!'

'Good night, sir', Gaston would say to a staggering customer he had just led gently but firmly to the door. 'See you tomorrow.' In the case of a woman it would be 'I look forward, madam, to the pleasure of your company tomorrow'. However, a heavily stoned Icelandic giant, who was vainly trying to obtain a drink at the bar one night, proved resistant to this civilised treatment. He not only refused to budge, but threatened to kill Gaston if he did not allow him to have a drink. His face was deadly white and his eyes glittered dangerously. I sensed that Gaston was frightened but he managed to assume a conciliatory smile,

The Last Lamplighter

albeit a rather sickly one. Nevertheless he stood his ground. The Icelandic hulk kept repeating his threat with increasing vehemence. As Gaston tried to pacify him he slowly backed towards the open door closely followed by his potential assassin. All of a sudden Gaston grabbed him by the shoulders, spun him round and gave him a violent shove that sent him lurching into the street. Then he slammed the door and bolted it.

Whenever he noticed that his bartenders were hard pressed, for whatever reason, he dived in to give them a hand. At closing time he would remove his jacket, roll up his sleeves and set about washing the dirty glasses. Interviewed one afternoon by a journalist for some magazine or other he suddenly excused himself and went off to collect empty glasses and deposit them on the counter. Then he returned to resume his interview.

John, a soppily idealistic young man, once asked Gaston to lend him ten shillings. 'Why should I lend you any money?' demanded Gaston. 'Last night you abused me for chucking out a drunken hooligan who was trying to pick a fight with one of my customers.' There was a pause. 'Oh well', he sighed. He drew out his wallet, extracted a ten-bob note and thrust it into the hand of the supplicant.

B. worked behind the bar at the French for about 15 years. He was sober, hard-working, intelligent and sociable. As a child he had undergone a minor operation on his face during the course of which the surgeon had accidentally severed a nerve. As a result his right cheek suffered partial paralysis. His speech was also impaired. In middle age he underwent an operation which, it was hoped, would repair the damage inflicted on him by the maladroit surgeon. It proved, alas, a total failure. B. took it badly and as a consequence sought consolation in drink.

Some Soho Characters

As soon as he arrived at the pub in the morning he would help himself to a stiff brandy and then discreetly tipple throughout the day. Towards the end of the evening he would stand behind the bar with glazed eyes endlessly wiping a glass with a towel in a slow, desultory manner. Customers could only gain his attention by making the most strenuous of efforts. Mindful of his physical disability, Gaston did not have the heart to sack him.

One day B. began to tell customers that he was having secret talks with President Reagan and Mao Tse Tung in order to bring about a reconciliation between the two leaders. Gaston persuaded him to enter a hospital for alcoholics where he was duly dried out and from which he was eventually discharged. There was no question of his going back to work at the French – or any pub, for that matter. Gaston gave him a golden handshake, although under no legal obligation to do so. The sum in question was £2,000. Shortly afterwards B. found a job as a newspaper vendor in Piccadilly Circus.

B. had rented from Gaston a room at the top of the building, which he left ankle-deep in empty beer cans, cigarette ends, old newspapers, dirty socks, half-eaten pork pies and hundreds of coins, most of them ten-penny pieces. An acrid smell of curry pervaded the room. It seems that B. sprinkled curry on the burgeoning litter to keep mice at bay. Gaston, typically, understood the heroic task of transferring the noxious rubbish to plastic bags and gave the room a thorough cleaning. He counted the coins and found they amounted to nearly £200.

Gaston had never been popular with Watney's, who owned the pub, for he declined to serve beer in pint glasses – 'My father didn't, so I don't' – install a fruit machine or clobber his customers with taped music. Moreover, when the licencing laws were relaxed to allow pubs to stay open in the afternoon he availed himself of the opportunity to do so, but perversely chose to close the bar at 9 o'clock at night. The brewers responded by upping his rent to a level he found unacceptable.

He chose to bow out on the 14th of July – Bastille Day. This was in 1989 when he was 75. From early afternoon until late evening the human overflow from the pub filled the street outside. Road blocks were erected by the police. The pub went dry about 7 o'clock and eventually closed. Shortly afterwards Gaston appeared at an open window on the first floor, presidential style, and waved at the crowd below. They responded with deafening, prolonged cheers. Eventually a moist-eyed Gaston moved away from the window. Several minutes later he was recalled by chants of 'Gaston! Gaston'. For the next hour the crowd recalled him to the window again and again. Finally he shouted down at them 'Go home, you lot!' and moved away from the window for the last time. The crowd gradually dispersed, leaving the street littered with empty wine bottles, discarded beer cans and cigarette butts.

Chicago, the black ex-boxer, became a 'regular' in the 50s. As a young middle-weight he had taken part in three world championships, though failing to gain any of the titles. One of his opponents had been Georges Carpentier. However, delectable compensation was afforded him in the form of Josephine Baker, the black music hall star, with whom he had an affair. He was living in Paris at that time. When age compelled him to abandon boxing he reluctantly took up all-in wrestling as a means of earning a crust. He was a member of the Club for Strong Men, which still exists and where a faded photograph of a young Chicago adorns one of the walls. After the fall of France he managed to escape to England. He rented a Victorian house in West London and took in lodgers. Some of them used to fall behind with their rent but Chicago, being a hopeless softy, allowed their arrears to accumulate. Into the bargain he lent money to indigent tenants. Before long he slid into the red and had to give up the house. He found a job as a chef in The Jungle, a posh West Indian restaurant in Soho. He continued to do work of this kind until his retirement. In his eighties he took over a newspaper pitch in Old Compton Street in order to supplement his old-age pension. He lived in a dosshouse in Covent Garden, where he was treated with affectionate respect by the inhabitants.

The north end of the French had been dubbed the 'deep end' by a waggish habitué, for poets and painters were wont to foregather there. The 'shallow end' to the south tended to be inhabited by copywriters and pornocrats. Night after night Chicago perched on the back of a chair – there were no stools in those days – at the end of the bar in the north where the artistic mob congregated. Broke most of the time, he cadged whiskies shamelessly from acquaintances, but when in funds distributed drinks to all and sundry with reckless prodigality.

His eyes were so soft and gentle that it was difficult to imagine him knocking the hell out of an opponent in the ring. He certainly fancied the ladies. When he was chatting with a dishy young thing, however, he was liable to subject her to a bear-like hug that sometimes caused bruisings. As a result victims of these contusing embraces took care to keep him at a respectable distance during conversations. An attractive 29-year old woman once told me she fancied him to such an extent that she could imagine herself going to bed with him. He was then 88. A male gospel singer from New York was grabbed by Chicago on one occasion and, to his extreme consternation, treated to a lascivious kiss.

The Last Lamplighter

In his late eighties Chicago began to suffer from arthritic knees. At the end of an especially bad day Gaston would hire a taxi to take him back to his dosshouse. During a spell in hospital Paul Potts visited him bearing a tattered paperback containing anecdotes about boxing stars of yesteryear. He departed clutching a half-bottle of whisky Chicago had bestowed on him.

When he was 93 Chicago took up residence in an old peoples' home in Paddington. Sohoites visited him bringing the obligatory bottle of whisky. He was once taken in a wheelchair to the Serpentine Gallery. The occasion was a private view of paintings by Craigie Aitchison, who had been a 'regular' years earlier. A young female acquaintance of Chicago glided over to kiss him lightly on his cheek. He immediately grabbed her with his brawny arms and, despite her squeaks of protest, pulled her down onto his knees.

At the age of 94 he went up to join Georges Carpentier and Josephine in the sky. I am sure they gave him a warm welcome.

As as young man Quentin Crisp was beautiful in an aristocratic though entirely unforbidding way. His appearance was effeminate, hennaed hair, lacquered fingernails, shoes with medium heels, but he was not in the least bit camp. Indeed, his behaviour in public was the model of propriety. He addressed everybody with mock formality by their surname preceded by Mr, Miss or Mrs. Alyson Stoneham Hunter, the short-story writer, who met him at a party in New York, told me she thought of him as a gentlewoman. A friend of mine worked in a West End bookshop where Quentin, now a celebrity, signed copies of his *Love Made Easy* one afternoon. The stint completed, he helped her to clear up his table. (He always had a bottle of wine at his elbow on these occasions.) Celebrities are not supposed to behave in this fashion and his demonstration of genuine humility impressed her enormously. He cheerfully lent me the odd half-crown during the war when I was broke. (Alas, they were never returned.) Maintaining, as he did, his outrageous appearance in those far-off illiberal days displayed courage of an outstanding order. The physical assaults he suffered at the hands of hooligans did not deter him in the least. Moreover, he made light of his injuries. His parting words were invariably 'Be terribly gay'. 'Gay' had not then been usurped by the homosexual fraternity.

Before the advent of the swinging 60s there were few eating places or clubs – he avoided pubs – where he was *persona grata*. One of these was the French café in Old Compton Street. However, it closed towards the end of the 50s. On the last day I saw him sitting on a stool near the entrance looking sad and remote. I encountered him one night in the Caves de France in Dean Street but he appeared to be untypically ill at ease and departed soon afterwards. I never saw him there again. One of his close acquaintances was 'Lamb Chop' Pulley, who eventually 'married' a director on the board of John Lewis. Quentin was told, no doubt gently, that he would not be a welcome visitor to their flat. Lamb Chop, moreover, stopped calling on him. They kept in touch by means of the telephone. Quentin accepted this arrangement uncomplainingly.

'Lamb Chop' had acquired his nickname in the early years of the war. Meat was then hard to come by, and Quentin had given him a couple of lamb chops which he bestowed on a prostitute who was plying her trade in Sloane Square. 'Thank you, darling' she said. 'My little dog will love these'. 'No he won't', snapped Pulley and grabbed them back. He related this incident to a friend of his who coined the sobriquet that henceforth clung to him.

Quentin once went on a day's outing to Canterbury with a married couple in their car. When they arrived in the city Quentin insisted on their going off without him as he did not want his bizarre appearance to embarrass them. Twenty minutes later he took a stroll around the city, making sure he did not run into them. Then he went back to the car to nibble at a bar of chocolate he had just bought and await the return of his friends.

One morning during the war I encountered Quentin in the King's Road pushing with considerable effort a bedstead whose castors squeaked piteously. Removal vans were then inconspicuous as petrol was severely rationed. So a spectacle of this kind was not unusual, at least in bohemian Chelsea. 'The angels will sing your praises forever, Mr Fothergill', he said as I came to his aid. I chose to be in front and guide the bedstead. Several minutes later we spotted an entirely sober Dylan Thomas on the opposite side of the road. He was pushing, with evident fatherly pride, a pram containing a peacefully snoozing baby. A hefty, rather plain Canadian woman, who lived above Quentin, helped us to manhandle the bedstead up the stairs and into his flat. Dust was accumulating steadily and would in the fulness of time achieve national fame. The Canadian lady, a devotee of Lesbos, was suffering, poor thing, from a hopeless passion for her beautiful neighbour.

The painter Peter Saunders once taught in an art school where Quentin was a model. 'I'm putty in your hands, Mr Saunders' he would say at the beginning of the class as he stood on the dais clad only in a jockstrap. He delighted in devising one-minute poses that were complex and convoluted. That he managed to maintain his balance during some of them seemed to Peter nothing less than a miracle. Having dressed at the end of a class, Quentin would often regale spellbound students with amusing, elegantly phrased anecdotes. On one occasion he wandered round the room inspecting the laborious efforts of the students. 'They're very nice indeed', he said, 'but it's all a waste of time really. At least I get paid for what I do.' Quentin affected to disdain Art, Poetry and Music to which, I suppose, he was merely indifferent. A friend of his, Barbara Norman, who wrote poetry, took against him eventually on this account and dropped him. He was redeemed, at least in my eyes, by his passion for movies.

During the 70s he visited New York, fell in love with the place and in time settled there. New Yorkers certainly loved him. L. D. Frazier, the huge Afro-American gospel singer, once told me that he and Quentin were strolling through the streets of New York one afternoon – they must have looked a strange couple – when he noticed that people were actually bowing to his companion as if he were royalty.

In a letter to me Quentin likens a visit to England to a sojourn in Alcatraz. It was the Mrs Grundy aspects of British life he disliked so intensely. As he boarded a red double-decker one morning a tiny little man piped up 'Why don't you git yer 'air cut?', but Quentin merely found this amusing.

I attended a one-man show of his one afternoon at the Duke of York's. It was strangely nostalgic to hear anecdotes he had retailed decades earlier in the Bar-B-Cue in King's Road. They had not lost their sparkle. During the interval he signed copies of his books in the foyer, chatted to his customers and sipped a glass of wine. He looked as if he were riding on the crest of a wave. We exchanged pleasantries before he dashed away to do the second half of the show. His parting words were 'Come to New York, where you will be happy forever!'

The Last Lamplighter

Julian MacLaren Ross (X. Trapnel in Anthony Powell's *A Dance to the Music of Time*) wore dark glasses that emphasised his hard jaw and thin lips, thereby giving him the appearance of a ruthless mafioso. Tall and upright, he carried a silver-topped cane and walked with a kind of stiff dignity. In winter he wore a fawn crombie overcoat and throughout the year a burgundy corduroy jacket. He smoked Royalty cigarettes through a holder as he talked endlessly in a monotonous, nasal voice about his vicissitudes as a writer. He was something of a bore. Yet his writings, mainly short stories and novels, were extremely entertaining. His *Memoirs of the Forties*, sadly uncompleted owing to his premature death, was no exception.

However, factual inaccuracies abound, while much of it is pure fiction. Not only, for instance, did he get Anthony Dickins's surname wrong, calling him Dickens, but he went on to state that he was a grandson of Charles Dickens. Also, referring to me as Steven, he maintained that I once locked Gerald Wilde and his painting materials in a room and only let him out when he had completed a painting. This only happened in Julian's lively imagination.

One night in the Wheatsheaf he declared that Fred Astaire was an Englishman. I was quite unable to disabuse him of this mistaken notion. On another occasion he referred to my 'drug addiction'. I assured him I was not a drug addict, which was true. 'But you were once', he said, 'and you're now cured'. I told him I had never been on drugs, which was also true. 'Yes, yes, you were a junky for a time', he insisted impatiently, 'and you kicked the habit'. At that point I gave up.

I told him one afternoon that I had been chucked out of the Duke of Wellington for not being in control of my legs. Thereafter he referred to me as Staggering Steven. In his memoirs he gives a graphic account of my drunken staggerings through the streets of Soho, which seemed to have impressed him deeply. Having left a pub at night in an exuberantly intoxicated condition, yet still in reasonable command of my legs, I would sometimes yield to the reckless impulse to execute Nijinsky-type leapings. As I left the ground each time I would punch the air savagely and utter barbaric yelps. It is a pity that Julian did not witness any of these performances, as I am sure he would have enjoyed them.

In the late 50s a play of his was performed on the Home Service, now known as Radio 4. About the same time Radio 3 broadcast a play by Philip O'Connor, the eccentric author of *Memoirs of a Public Baby*. One afternoon they met by chance in a bank, whither they had repaired to cash their respective cheques from the Corporation. When Philip learnt that Julian's was larger than his he made harsh, twanging noises in his throat. These denoted wounded feelings and extreme annoyance. Julian told me later in the Wheatsheaf that he thought Philip possessed the superior talent of the two and had suffered an injustice. This demonstration of literary humility was pleasantly unexpected.

I first met Frank Norman in the early 50s in a Cypriot café in Charlotte Street. He was a morose young Cockney with a razor scar on his left cheek. He had a handsome Afro-English girl friend. They were both on their uppers and so I put them up for a couple of weeks. Desperate for dosh Frank, unbeknownst to me, pinched a porcelain vase belonging to a painter who had a room on the same floor as mine. The vase, incidentally, was of no great value.

Eventually a rich woman rescued Frank from his life of

poverty and insecurity. During this period he wrote *Bang To Rights*, an account in racy Cockney of his prison experiences. Raymond Chandler contributed a preface to the book. He went on to write two more books consisting of reminiscences of his life at the bottom of the social heap. Then he and Lionel Bart wrote a musical entitled *Fings Ain't Wot They Used T'Be*. It was staged at the Garrick Theatre, where it proved to be a smash hit and ran for several years.

Frank was now rolling. 'This is a better lark than tea-leafing', he declared one night in the French. By way of illustration he proudly exhibited for my benefit a gold bracelet, gold cigarette case and lighter, and a gold wristwatch. He treated his boozing companions in Soho to similar ludicrous displays, but their cool response soon persuaded him to abandon the practice.

One evening in the same pub I happened to be standing next to Frank and a young German woman. Suddenly Frank began to talk in angry tones. I heard him refer to her as a typical Hun. I butted in to upbraid him for the despicable nature of his insult. He reacted by telling me I was a nobody. 'If you're a somebody', I retorted, 'I'm glad I'm a nobody'.

However, these were the only unfriendly words we ever exchanged over the years. I had a soft spot for Frank, who was almost invariably genial, ebullient and amusing. In time I came to think of him as a redoubtable old trouper.

He sometimes brought up the subject of the stolen vase, but I always told him it was a mere peccadillo committed by him in the distant past when he was young and irresponsible. Besides, he had abandoned his nefarious activities shortly after this incident, finding they dominated his mental processes to the virtual exclusion of everything else. He certainly avoided villains like the plague. However, there was one exception in the form of Brian the Burglar. Like Frank he was warm-hearted and good fun. They encountered each other one day in the Swiss pub, where Brian told Frank that he had been released from Pentonville Prison that very morning after doing a spell of bird. Frank immediately drew out his wallet, extracted a ten-pound note and thrust it into Brian's breast pocket. 'I know what it's like', he said.

'Fuck this Cockney lark,' he said one day. 'I'm going to learn to write in the Queen's English. And he did just that. He was no doubt helped by his wife, Geraldine, who was a saleroom correspondent of The Times. They were an unlikely couple, but it was a happy marriage. The first fruit of his labours was *Banana Boy*, an account of his life in a Barnardo's Home. After that, it was mainly novels. They have style, panache and good plots, but lack psychological interest.

He once boasted to me that he had lived on the proceeds from his writing ever since the publication of *Bang To Rights*. He worked hard during the week and on Friday evenings descended on Soho for booze-ups. The subsequent hangovers laid him low for the next two days.

In his early fifties he contracted Hodgkins disease. He put up a plucky fight but lost.

Signor Fava was an elderly, bewigged, fierce-looking gentleman who had been a member of the chorus at the Milan Opera House before the war. There was a noticeable gap between his wig and the hairline at the back of his head. He owned a little café in Greek Street in the late 40s. Laconic and unsmiling, he served his customers from behind a counter. On Sunday afternoons an accordionist and a guitar player delivered Neapolitan melodies. At about 4 o'clock Signor Fava emerged from behind the counter with a mandolin and seated himself with an air of great solemnity between the two musicians. Having tuned his mandolin he sang three or four Neapolitan songs in a harsh, uncertain voice to his own accompaniment. I was fascinated by his playing, which had a ferocious intensity. Indeed, I almost expected sparks to fly off his instrument. As he returned one day to his counter after one of these performances, the guitarist began to quietly strum a Cole Porter tune. Signor Fava spun round and glared at him. 'I donna want no jungle music in 'ere', he barked.

'Weer 'e all queer as coots, yer noo', Robert MacBryde confided to me one night in the Swiss pub. He was referring to Robert Colquhoun and himself. Known in Soho as the Roberts, they were Scottish painters who, at that time in the early 40s, were riding high in the art world. But I had known they were homosexuals – actually Colquhoun was bisexual – and lived together in the manner of a married couple with MacBryde in the role of wife. Colquhoun's penchant for females, not unnaturally, caused problems between the two men. An attractive young woman with a compelling tragic look used to hang around Colquhoun, which greatly displeased MacBryde. In time, however, he began to feel sorry for the wretched creature and eventually allowed her to share their bed. She was now an exceedingly happy young woman, but having lost her tragic aspect, looked rather ordinary.

MacBryde had a warm, affectionate, life-loving nature. At the drop of a hat he would regale one with old Scottish songs in a soft, lilting voice. It has been said he had a malicious side but I never encountered it. Colquhoun possessed a fair intellect, a sardonic sense of humour and lean good looks that fascinated women.

On pub crawls together MacBryde liked to stay close to Colquhoun, who found this irritating and would tell him to fuck off. The latter would protest, sometimes in whimpering tones, but then a major row would erupt that often ended in a fight. Bruce Bernard, who these days produces art books among other things, was a friend of the Roberts. One afternoon he was drinking with them in the Coach and Horses when they had one of their notorious punch-ups. As a consequence Annie, the publican's wife, barred them. She also banned Bruce simply for being with them, which he felt was distinctly unfair.

One evening I wandered into the French pub in a state of extreme dejection. I was vaguely aware of the Roberts standing near the bar. 'Yer look as if yer need a wee whisky', said Colquhoun. Moments later I was holding a glass of whisky. After I had gratefully downed the inspiring liquid, MacBryde replenished my glass. As a young man Bruce had once undergone a severe emotional crisis, which made it difficult for him to cope with life. The Roberts helped him to weather the storm and even put him up for a time.

'Bruce is going up north again', MacBryde informed me one day with a chuckle. In those days Bruce had a habit of quitting the Soho scene to go up to a northern town to live and work. Perhaps he found northerners more honest, less pretentious and warmer-hearted than Londoners. As young men are apt to do, he was doubtless seeking a spiritual home (Paris and St Ives had been found wanting). But the north failed to fulfil that role and he eventually returned to London for good.

In the 50s the Roberts began to find it difficult to sell their paintings and gradually declined into alcoholism. I once encountered them lurching down Berwick Street as they scoffed fish-and-chips out of newspaper wrappings. The spectacle rather shocked me. On another occasion a policeman arrested MacBryde in Dean Street for being drunk and disorderly. He unwisely put up a fight. The policeman pinioned one of his arms behind his back, informed him he intended to break the limb and proceeded to do so. Bernard Farmer, the abstract painter and erstwhile jazz drummer, first met MacBryde one night in the French. MacBryde was homeless at the time and so Bernard allowed him to spend the night at his flat. Bernard arose on the following morning to find that MacBryde had departed, having urinated on his bed and even his record player. Later that day Bernard ran into MacBryde in the French pub and greeted him coldly. But MacBryde stared at him without a glimmer of recognition. It was a genuine case of amnesia.

Conan Nicholas, the journalist, once threw a party in his house which the Roberts attended. After the other guests had left, they hung around hoping Conan would put them up. But he told them he had no intention of doing so. Angry protests resulted. He had almost physically to eject them. As he was closing the front door, MacBryde pointed an accusing finger at him. 'Yer the *hell* of England', he shouted.

MacBryde was inconsolable after the death of Colquhoun, whose dicky heart had finally given up. Night after night in the French pub he would murmur drunkenly to himself over and over again 'Arv lost ma lover'. Somebody cruelly referred to him as a professional widow. But his grief was real. He eventually went to live in Dublin, where he began to recover and paint again. One day however, he was knocked down by a car and killed.

Archer, as he was known to his friends, was one of Soho's most endearing characters. Invariably attired in a suit, erect, bespectacled and looking rather fierce at times, he suggested an authoritarian headmaster of a public school. But appearances can be misleading, and Archer, in fact, was a kindly man with a wry sense of humour and a tendency to erupt occasionally into loud laughter. He always carried a few books or magazines under his right arm, which was crippled. In this way he gave his arm something to do and at the same time camouflaged his disability. He used the word 'vaguely' a great deal. Thus he would say he was feeling 'vaguely cheerful' or 'vaguely squiffy' or 'vaguely wilted'. On one notable occasion he declared he was feeling 'vaguely shattered'. Sometimes he would say he was 'vaguely ebbing', which meant he was about to shove off.

In the early 30s he opened a bookshop in Bloomsbury, and later published books under the imprint of the Parton Press. He seemed to have a flair for spotting poetic talent for he put out the first books of Dylan Thomas (*18* Poems), George Barker, David Gascoyne and W. S. Graham. However, he was less successful as a bookseller since he gave away large numbers of his books – he seemed positively to dislike selling them – and studiously avoided boring chores like stocktaking or checking accounts. Thus he fell heavily into debt and had eventually to close the shop. In the 50s he opened another one, this time in Greek Street, Soho, but it failed for the same reasons.

Although he probably had an instinct about good poets, I suspect he liked the idea of poetry rather more than the stuff itself. An earnest young man in a duffle coat buttonholed him one night in the French. He declared that he was a poet and began to declaim one of his efforts at a stony-faced Archer. Suddenly Archer exclaimed: 'Oh, do stop it. I can't *stand* poetry'.

He had a private income of sorts, much of which ended up in the pockets of impecunious poets and artists. As so often recounted, there was a period when he was wont to put a banknote into an empty matchbox and slip it into the pocket of a needy friend, whom he wished to spare embarrassment. It is possible that some of these beneficiaries threw their matchbox away under the impression that it was empty. Whenever he was broke himself, he would apply to his father, Major Archer, for a spot of lolly, and invariably received it. His obliging parent owned a large country estate, which he had eventually to sell off, acre by acre, to raise money for his profligate son.

Archer was a homosexual, who from time to time 'had a thing' about some young man or other. But nothing ever came of these infatuations. 'Silly billy me', he would say rather sadly on those occasions. He once had a crush on a working class youth who was married. It was all quite hopeless, not least because Archer, being a thoroughly decent person, would have done nothing to endanger this relationship. So he lavished money and gifts on the youth – on both of them in fact – and suffered.

He was always keen that 'straight' friends of his who were unmarried should rectify the omission. (I sometimes felt that Archer had a secret yearning for a conventional life). 'I'm frightfully worried about Bruce', he confided to me one day. 'It really is time he settled down. After all he's knocking forty. We must all jolly well put our heads together and do a spot of foxy matchmaking'. Bruce, I suspect, represented for him a surrogate son.

Archer eventually exhausted his private income, and in time father ran out of saleable acres. Before long Archer found himself down to his last penny and then, to everybody's surprise, found a job at Selfridges as a sales assistant in the electrical department. Typically, he tried to set up a 'cultural group' in the store, but the scheme failed through lack of support from members of the staff. I admired his courage in taking on a job, which, although entirely worthy, would have been considered unsuitable by conventional people for a man of his class and generation. And, of course, Archer was far from happy selling reading lamps and wall sockets.

'My friends keep telling me how marvellous I am doing this job', he once confided to me. 'And why doesn't somebody find me a job on the Arts Council? It makes me absolutely furious'. He said he was feeling 'terribly edgy' and had to go for a walk. He returned half-an-hour later looking comparatively calm and breathing normally. He often had occasions in those days to go on a therapeutic mini walkabout.

He eventually left Selfridges to embark on a career as a full-time cadger. (In view of the vast sums of money he had given away over the decades one could hardly censure him for reversing roles). He wrote begging letters to affluent public figures and tapped Soho acquaintances, all of which seemed to him at first like an amusing game.

He was sitting one night at a table in the French with Paul Potts, no mean tapper himself, and therefore a serious rival. Suddenly Archer spotted a well-heeled Sohoite entering the pub. He instantly sprang to his feet and made a beeline for him. Having so smartly staked his claim, he smiled at Paul mischievously. Paul looked very cross indeed.

One evening I was walking down Dean Street with Paul who, I felt sure, would ask me for a loan at any moment, when Archer unexpectedly joined us. Aware of the threat to his chances of a successful touch, Paul acted decisively. 'Fuck off, Archer', he said. 'Oh, really', protested Archer. Nevertheless he obediently 'ebbed'.

One afternoon in the French Archer noticed a rich female acquaintance of his sitting in a corner. He immediately swooped on her. 'I suppose you're skint as usual', she said wearily. However, she eventually softened and slipped him something. Archer thanked her profusely and departed. Several minutes later he returned brandishing a bunch of flowers, which he presented to her with a gallant bow. 'Archer, you're utterly ridiculous', she protested. 'No, I *don't* want a drink, you silly old sod'. I occasionally lent him a pound, only to be given a cheque for two or three pounds a week or so later. It was useless to protest.

In time, the cadging lark began to lose its glamour for him and he came to the bitter conclusion that life had treated him scurvily. One often heard him say he was 'absolutely furious' about something or other. 'Friends of mine have organized a fund for me but they dole it out in small amounts as if I were a child. It makes me absolutely furious'. 'I used to sell copies of Dylan's *18 Poems* for 3/6 each. These days one of them is worth £500. It makes me absolutely furious'. 'I was 60 yesterday. It makes me absolutely furious'. One evening in a friend's flat he was sitting in an armchair knocking back brandies and being 'absolutely furious' about various things, when she noticed with alarm that steam was rising from his balding pate. She swore to me she had not imagined it.

His friends eventually began to tire of his continual demands for money and many of them declined to cough up. The trust withered away. Life for Archer became decidedly ribby. He moved into a room in a Salvation Army hostel in the East End. To add to his miseries he contracted arthritis, which causes him considerable pain and compelled him to walk with a stick.

One night I encountered him in the Swiss, a pub in Old Compton Street, where he was standing alone near the entrance. He was looking ill and shabby. He greeted me briskly but then produced a bottle of aspirins and said: 'Do you think these will do the trick?' I was stunned for a few moments. Recently he had been talking about going to live in Brighton, where he had friends. I plugged the town for all I was worth but, sadly, encountered solid sales resistance. He mentioned Bruce who was still unmarried, and said he was terribly worried about him. Then he bade me farewell and departed.

Appalled, I dashed out of the pub in search of him. But he was nowhere to be seen.

He returned to his room in the hostel that night, wrote a few letters and then put an end to himself.

Some days later as I was standing in the bar of the French, a member of the staff gave me a letter. It was from Archer. In it he said that by the time it reached me he would be dead. He was glad, it seemed, to have seen me that night, and he expressed a wish that things would go well with me. He went on to say that he would have done it two days earlier but on that day he'd run into an old friend of his who had given him £10, and he felt he ought to spend it.

W. S. Graham, the Scottish poet, known to his friends as Sidney, grew up in Glasgow but left it during the war to settle in London. Shortly after his arrival I met him one afternoon in the Swiss pub. He was sitting alone at a table, gazing with awe at a small figure with dishevelled hair and bloodshot eyes, who was standing at the bar. This was his first sight of Dylan Thomas in the flesh. He told me he intended to introduce himself to the Welsh poet as soon as he could summon up enough courage to do so. After a few minutes he downed the remains of his glass of bitter and stood up. 'Here goes', he declared and took the plunge.

Sidney soon became a familiar face in Soho. He had rugged features, physical grace and attractively taut Glaswegian vowels. He wore an old tweed jacket and baggy flannels.

The Last Lamplighter

He stayed for a time with Bobby Hunt in his South London flat. The latter was then an art student, who later illustrated books and launched a photographic library. Until recently he played a punchy trumpet in an amateur jazz band. Amiably manic, he is the fastest talker I have ever known. Bobby's father, appropriately enough, was a bobby for whom he had a great affection.

Bobby and Sidney were often broke and hungry. One day the latter devised a plan to provide each of them with a free meal. First of all he picked up at a local butcher's shop a few mutton bones that would otherwise have been thrown away. Then he called on a neighbour and said he wanted to make an Irish stew and had all the necessary vegetables except potatoes. Would it be possible...? The neighbour cheerfully gave him a few spuds. Sidney knocked on the door of another neighbour and said he wanted to make an Irish stew and had all the necessary vegetables except carrots. Would it be possible...? The neighbour duly obliged. In this way Sidney gradually acquired all the vegetables he needed for the stew.

Early one morning they were walking through a deserted shopping centre in South London on their way home from a party when they were stopped by a policeman – not Bobby's father as it happened. In the late 40s it was unusual to see anybody in the street in this part of the capital at 5 o'clock in the morning, except, that is, policemen, burglars and lamplighters. Yielding to an impulse to be facetious, Sidney said they were both out of work and looking at advertisements for job vacancies in shop windows, having decided to make an early start. The policeman accepted this absurd explanation and allowed them to proceed on their way.

Sidney was always a drinker but in time became a dedicated one. As a result his sartorial standards, never high at

Some Soho Characters

the best of times, declined even further. One evening he turned up at the BBC Television Centre – this was in the 60s – to give a live interview. However, the commissionaire mistook him for a tramp and refused to allow him into the building. Sidney remonstrated with him but in vain. The commissionaire could not believe that the scruffy figure before him was a famous poet shortly due to appear on millions of television screens throughout the country. Fortunately the interviewer, an extremely worried young man by now, happened to look out of a window and spotted Sidney standing around in the courtyard below. He dashed down to claim him for his programme with only minutes in hand.

In 1950 or thereabouts Sidney and his wife, Nessie, moved to Cornwall, where he found a job as a coastguard. He published collections of his poems. However, an excessive devotion to whisky eventually caused his muse to desert him for several years.

I encountered them one evening in the French pub in the early 80s. At least 30 years must have passed since I last saw them. Nessie seemed to have changed little but a grey-haired Sidney undoubtedly showed his age. His blotchy complexion, sadly, testified to his love of the bottle. Whereas, however, he had been uptight in the old days he was now relaxed and sociable with a touch of the pub performer about him. As I chatted with him the image of a young Sidney kept superimposing itself on the face before me, which was a strange experience. Towards the end of the evening he placed his hands affectionately on my shoulders – and regaled me with a popular sentimental ditty of yesteryear. This was the last time I ever saw him.

I had always thought of Francis Bacon as being tall but I observed him in the French one afternoon leaning against the bar and realised that this was not the case. Indeed his legs were rather short. I first set eyes on him towards the end of the war in the Black Horse in Rathbone Place, which he frequented in those days. At the time he affected make-up and artificially blonde hair. I did not meet him until several years later. I was drinking with Colquhoun one afternoon in Les Caves de France in Dean Street when Bacon came over to chat with him. He had considerable charm and a courteous manner that belonged to an older, more civilized world. He told Robert, who by then had become a full-time drinker, that he thought it was a pity that he was no longer painting.

When John Deakin, the photographer, was dying of cancer, Bacon arranged for him to stay at an hotel in Brighton and settled the bills. One night he ran into a forlorn-looking Jeffrey Bernard in the street: 'I suppose you're broke as usual', he said and stuffed several fifty-pound notes into his breast pocket. Francis dropped into the French shortly after it had been taken over by Noel Botham and Lesley Lewis and introduced himself to them. Then he bought a bottle of champagne and invited them to share it with him.

But he had a black side that emerged during bouts of heavy drinking. Daniel Farson, the photographer and close friend of Bacon's, no mean boozer himself, lurched into the French one evening looking distressed. He told me he had just been subjected to a verbal assault from Francis that had been vicious and prolonged. Tears rolled down his cheeks as he recounted this painful experience. Yet it is only fair to add that Francis apologized to him on the following day.

One night in Groucho's Francis began to abuse Jay Landesman, the American publisher and author of two books of memoirs, who retaliated in kind. Suddenly Francis grabbed him by the lapels of his jacket in Bogart fashion and accidentally tore a button. Overcome by remorse he somehow managed to conjure up a needle and spool of thread and sewed the button back on. Then they hugged each other in an access of drunken sentimentality.

Jay dressed with considerable care in a style that verged on the flamboyant. One afternoon I came upon him lying flat on his back on the pavement outside Gerry's in Dean Street. He had passed out after knocking back several drinks on an empty stomach. Despite, however, his abrupt transition from a vertical position to a horizontal one, he had retained his immaculate appearance. Even his Panama hat was perfectly in position. Two Sohoites I knew appeared on the scene and we hauled him to his feet. Within minutes he was rolling homewards in a taxi.

He was a self-proclaimed philanderer. One night in the French he found himself standing next to an attractive young woman at the bar. He did not beat about the bush. 'I'm Jay,' he said. 'How about I buy a bottle of champagne and we boogie on down to my pad?' The woman was amused by his direct approach but declined the invitation. Another night in the same pub I was chatting with an attractive girl with no ulterior motive in mind when he sauntered past. He smiled at me encouragingly and whispered: 'You godda winner there, kid'.

His wife, Fran, wrote sophisticated lyrics for tunes with a jazzy flavour. One of these was the famous *Spring Hangs You Up The Most*, which was recorded by Ella Fitzgerald. The couple left New York in the early 60s to settle down in London. They threw a party every year on New Year's Eve which was attended by virtually the whole of bohemian Soho.

Tony's was undoubtedly the sleaziest café in Fitzrovia yet also the most popular. Situated in Charlotte Street it was known as 91. George, a Maltese gentleman, was the part-time owner, his face disfigured by razor scars. Despite his sinister appearance, he was a kindly, family man. The customers consisted mainly of bohemians, small-time villains and prostitutes with hard faces. They tended to favour the ground floor in the daytime but at night the basement usually filled up. One afternoon a youthful Lucian Freud strode into the café and jocularly ordered the customers to make way for the grandson of Sigmund Freud.

Dylan Thomas sometimes made an unsteady descent to the basement after the local pubs had closed at 10.30. He was usually accompanied by boozing companions that included Louis MacNeice, Elizabeth Lutyens, Edward Clark (the dapper promoter of atonal music), and BBC producers of Radio 3 drama. Thus the basement had a certain artistic ambience. One night Dylan brought down a Welsh rugger team who gloriously belted out songs of their native land.

I first met Jeffrey Bernard down there. A mere 15-year-old, he was attired in a naval cadet's uniform. Despite his tender years, however, he displayed an impressive gift of the gab.

One evening I was sitting around in the basement with Jeff and his two brothers Oliver and Bruce, and Vernon Scannell. Jeff was by now a fully fledged bohemian and worked at a night bakery. Oliver, the eldest of the brothers, was wielding a pneumatic drill on a building site and writing poems. Bruce was a student at St Martin's. Vernon had been a professional boxer and was now teaching literature somewhere and writing poetry. For some reason a row broke out between him and Jeff, who told him to get to his feet and put up his fists. This was extremely foolhardy and it was all over in a few seconds.

Perhaps Bruce thought that the honour of the Bernards

was at stake for he encountered Vernon in the Wheatsheaf one day and invited him to step outside. He fared no better than his younger brother.

Another habitué of the basement was Ken Richmond, the famous wrestler, who biffs the gong at the start of many Rank movies of the 40s and 50s. My previous girl friend ditched me in favour of this handsome hulk. He eventually joined the Jehovah's Witnesses. His formidable appearance must have ensured that his door-to-door proselytising was highly successful.

Ray Courtens was known as Canadian Ray. He was small and slight with furrowed features and lively intelligent eyes. He had a sunny, ebullient nature. When anybody inflicted on him views he considered obnoxious or merely absurd he responded with gentle mocking humour. For years he toiled on a novel. The completed manuscript ran to over 500 pages. One afternoon in Tony's I read a chapter. The style had obviously been influenced by the novels of Thomas Wolfe but I was impressed by the richness of the prose in those few pages. Alas, the book was never published. During a visit to Paris he consigned it to the Seine. This marked the end of his writing life.

He resolutely declined to engage in gainful employment and survived by scrounging. He slept on the floors of friends. Sometimes he spent the night in a bombed building. Pentonville Prison put him up for a few weeks. It seems that he had defied a court order to send alimony to his estranged wife. One night he hid himself in the lavatory in the backyard of Tony's as the café was about to close. He waited until he was sure that everybody had departed and then climbed through the half-opened window of the kitchen and raided the larder.

Pot smoking in those days was mainly confined to West

The Last Lamplighter

Indians, the bop crowd and a few bohemians. For Ray it was a way of life. Indeed he smoked it incessantly. To have afforded this pastime he must have done a spot of pushing.

In time the drug affected his mind. He grew a long beard and began to spout passages from the Gospels. One day he circumcised himself with an old razor blade. About the same time a Jewish friend of his, a drug pedlar and petty thief, had a plastic operation on his nose. Thus they knocked about Fitrovia together, one with a bandaged nose, the other with a bandaged penis.

Shortly afterwards he disappeared from Fitrovia. I later learnt he was living in the country with a divorced woman and her three children. He never returned to his bohemian haunts.

Jimmy the Baker, who had grown up in the Catholic area of Belfast, had a battered, handsome face, a shock of white hair, and limped badly. As a child he had dashed heedlessly into a busy road and been knocked down by a lorry which crushed his right foot. It seems his parents did not consider this sufficient punishment for his momentary neglect of road safety and confiscated his violin, which he played with loving dedication.

He was a kindly, decent man with a stoical attitude to life and a wry sense of humour. He played chess with considerable skill. One night in a pub he became involved in an argument with a young lout who made a sneering reference to his disability. Suddenly all the bitterness he had suppressed for so many years erupted violently. He attacked the miserable creature in a state of blind fury and nearly killed him. As a consequence he resolved never to touch another drop of drink. Thereafter he confined his social life to cafés.

Jeff Bernard, recently a labourer on a building site and a

kitchen porter, once told me that working in a bakery had been the hardest job he had ever done: the intense physical exertion, the appalling heat from the ovens and the long nocturnal hours. When Jimmy was knocking 60 he gave it up to sell newspapers in the street.

By then Fitzrovia had disappeared and Soho cafés were closing due to soaring rents. One afternoon I ran into Jimmy in Old Compton Street. He told me there were no longer any cafés in Soho where he could meet old cronies and chat over endless cups of tea. I mentioned a couple of pubs where he would find a few of those familiar faces but he declared that nothing would induce him to enter a pub. We drifted into the Bar Italia, mainly inhabited by Italians in those days. We had a coffee, chatted for a while in a forlorn sort of way and parted from each other. I never saw him in Soho again. I sometimes visited him in Upper Regent Street where he had a pitch. One day I found it occupied by a stranger. It seems that Jimmy had fallen ill and been taken to a hospital where he died shortly afterwards.

Redvers Gray, another habitué of 91, had a hawk-like nose and a fierce jutting beard. His voice was nasal and harsh. He wore a weather-beaten trilby and most of the year an old overcoat encircled by a leather belt. He rode around on a true tricycle. His invariable greeting to me was: 'Ah, Mr Fothergill, whom the Almighty One continues to preserve'. He was a defrocked solicitor. Years earlier he had fallen foul of the law by obtaining a false passport for a refugee woman. It was an act of pure chivalry for which he had received no payment.

His head teemed with ideas for inventions, none of which he managed to translate into reality. One day he was working on a cigarette case that was meant to produce a flame when opened, and set fire to his beard. For a time he was obsessed by the idea of floating soap. A friend of his allowed him to use her bathroom as a laboratory. He virtually lived there for a few weeks, which drove the poor woman up the wall. He finally abandoned his dream of floating soap. He then renounced invention in favour of artistic creation. He began to make collages which consisted of crushed peaches stuck to squares of cardboard. However, they failed to take the art world by storm.

For a while he lived in a room on the top floor of a bombed house in Fitzroy Street. There was no roof so he erected a large umbrella under which he cooked meals on a primus stove and kipped in a sleeping bag.

He eventually abandoned Fitzrovia to settle down in the country and work as a gardener.

John Williams – Williams not Millions he insisted – was a merchant seaman during the war and later a postal worker. In the 40s and 50s he haunted gambling dens in Soho, where he played poker and dice. All of them were illegal and most of them sleazy. One establishment that aspired to gentility with its carpeted floor, shaded lights and so on, was frequented by local gangsters. John visited the place when a game of dice was in progress. Before his first throw he vociferously invoked the aid of the Almighty in the approved fashion. The mobsters at the table instantly shushed him in shocked tones. Mysteriously, the place was never raided by the police.

John was shooting dice in a gambling den of a strictly basic type when the police descended on it. The occupants of the room were rounded up and taken in a police van to West End Central. The sergeant in charge of the operation told them they could play dice while waiting for their finger prints to be taken. This they proceeded to do, albeit in a subdued manner. Adopting the practise of the 'croupier' in gambling dens, the sergeant claimed 10 per cent of the winnings.

Bryce MacNabb, who worked for a film company as a reader, was another notable eccentric. A small, prematurely elderly gentleman with fierce blue eyes and a purple nose, he wore a battered old trilby, a well-worn tweed jacket and baggy flannels whose crotch seemed in danger of slipping down to his knees. As he stood stiff-necked at the bar of the French pub he had an air of a haughty Edwardian toff compelled to endure the company of social inferiors. He scorned to wear socks believing that feet needed lots of air. Instead he sprinkled the insides of his shoes with face powder, which served to absorb perspiration. Concealed under the arch of his left foot was a matchbox containing a roll of banknotes. By this means he hoped to outwit potential pickpockets and muggers. He liked to drink bitter, laced occasionally with whisky, but always left a small amount of liquor at the bottom of every glass, presumably to denote breeding. For some reason he habitually spoke in a quiet voice that sometimes sank to a whisper. This meant that anyone of medium height or more had to bend down to catch what he was saying. One night a tall habitué of the French pub approached me massaging the back of his neck. 'I've just been under Bryce's hat', he informed me wryly.

During the war Bryce had been a fireman in the Auxiliary Fire Service, an unlikely occupation for so dignified a personage. One night he and his fellow firefighters had just tackled a blazing building when a member of the Luftwaffe came floating down out of the sky to land a few yards from where they were standing. Some of the firemen unsheathed their axes with the vengeful intention of shortening the life of the wretched German. Bryce, however, interposed himself between the German, a mere boy, and his potential killers. 'Do not harm this man', he commanded. 'He is now my prisoner and I intend to escort him to the nearest police station'. This he proceeded to do.

Bryce was married to Netta, a calm, pleasant, intelligent woman who had been the wife of the novelist, Richard Aldington. During her second marriage she had a brief affair with Dylan Thomas. At that time she and Bryce were living in Kensington, while Dylan was staying with friends in Bayswater. Bryce's reaction to her aberrant behaviour was a trifle unusual. 'I don't in the least mind your having an affair with Dylan', he declared one day, 'but, hang it all, the fellow lives on the wrong side of the park'. One morning as she was emerging from her bath – Bryce had been sponging her back – she asked him if he did not think she still had a good figure. 'You have a good figure', he said, 'for a man of my age'.

Neal Perrot, their GP and friend, sometimes dropped over to their flat for lunch on a Sunday. During these meals, however, Bryce would merely sit at the table imbibing wine and making conversation. On one of these occasions Neal commented on the fact that he had never seen Bryce eating. 'Some people are secret drinkers', said Bryce, 'I am a secret eater'. On another occasion Bryce announced with a mischievous gleam in his eye that he was going to ring up a certain titled lady of his acquaintance, whom, it seemed, he rather disliked. He dialled her number and waited for a few moments. Then he enquired 'Is that Miss Whiplash? I hear that you offer reduced rates on Sunday afternoons'. There was the sound of an angry female voice and Bryce returned the receiver to its cradle with a chuckle.

He was apt to hit male customers who insulted him. One night in the French, M., a notorious troublemaker, thought

Some Soho Characters

he would have a bit of fun winding up Bryce. He went too far, however, when he told Bryce he thought he was a self-important, bourgeois hack. Bryce reddened, rose on his toes and appeared to swell in the manner of certain animals under attack. Then he delivered a right-hander to the jaw of his persecutor, who staggered back a few paces and in so doing transferred most of the red wine in his glass to the front of his shirt. Gaston descended on M. and eyed him sternly for a moment. 'Good night Sir', he said, and shepherded him to the door.

Bryce liked to indulge in doom talk from time to time. It might be, according to him, the imminence of a nuclear holocaust or the inevitable extinction of life on the planet through pollution. Another theme was the insatiable demand of trade unions for pay rises that would cause rampant inflation and the eventual collapse of the economy. 'There is no hope', he would intone mournfully, 'Absolutely none. No hope whatsoever'. Trying to disabuse him of these doom-laden notions was, I found, a fruitless exercise. In a fit of exasperation one day I told him I felt that he was a self-indulgent pessimist. My rebuke offended him deeply but it appeared not to merit a right-hander.

In a state of alcoholic euphoria he would sometimes croon *Too Many Rings Around Rosie* which was a tune from *No, No Nanette*, a musical comedy of the twenties. As he did so he swayed from side to side wearing a beatific smile. He would then execute a kind of modified soft shoe shuffle which he concluded with a triumphal 'You betcha!' Moments later he became again the haughty Edwardian toff.

As he stood at the bar one evening he related an anecdote about his falling into the Hythe Canal in the thirties attired in plus fours on which dry cleaners later inflicted a knife-edged crease. But then his mood appeared to change and his face acquired a baleful expression. All of a sudden he whipped off his trilby, thereby revealing a shiny bald pate, and subjected it to a series of vicious punches. Then he hurled it at the ceiling allowing it to fall to the ash-strewn floor. A savage kick sent it flying into the street. Having retrieved it he returned to the pub looking deeply remorseful. He dusted it carefully with the back of his hand and gravely replaced it on his head.

Bryce and I had emerged from the French pub one night at closing time and were walking past the posh Italian restaurant next door when he suddenly came to a halt. 'Hold on', he said as he stared at the window with an air of marked disapproval. Then he began to mimic a window cleaner at work making broad sweeping movements across the surface of the glass. Diners seated at a table near the window were visibly startled. All of a sudden he affected to notice a bad spot and pretended to rub away at it vigorously. Finally he stepped back to survey the window. 'One of my better efforts I rather feel', he said with an air of deep satisfaction.

One day Netta died unexpectedly of a heart attack. Bryce was devastated. He had given up his bread-and-butter job in the movie world but made another start on a book he had been toiling on for years. This was a prose poem, or something of the kind, based on his traumatic experiences in the AFS. In time, however, he began to weary of the daily, seemingly endless struggle with words. The French pub, moreover, was now full of noisy, jostling young people who largely ignored him. Above all, he continued to grieve for Netta. He decided it was time to go.

He simply took to his bed and stopped eating. Concerned friends of his visited him and tried to persuade him to take nourishment but to no avail. He did, however, accept drinks.

Some Soho Characters

So friends dropped in with bottles of whisky and beer and macabre parties took place. At the funeral service one of the mourners reverentially placed Bryce's battered old trilby on the coffin before it disappeared into the oven.

Lamplighting and Georgia on My Mind

In the early 50s I became obsessed by a romantic dream of playing a smoochy jazz trumpet in a smoky night club. So I hire-purchased a trumpet, a gleaming, brand-new copper-plated affair of which I was extremely proud. My theatre jobs gave me all the time I needed for practising the instrument but they were poorly paid. At that time a painter friend of mine, Hal Woolf, was working as a lamplighter for the North Thames Gas Board. The streets of London in those days were illuminated at night mainly by gas lamps. He told me the Board treated the job as a full-time one and paid their employees accordingly, but in practise it involved only a few hours of graft every day. For this reason I decided the job would suit me admirably for a time.

The Board's headquarters were in Westminster. My interviewer informed me that lamplighters were paid £4 for a week consisting of seven days. He then presented me with a form in which I had, among other things, to state that all my limbs were intact, that I could ride a bicycle, and that I did not suffer from vertigo. I filled in the form to his satisfaction. He seemed more than willing to offer me a job. In those days of virtually full employment he must have had

Lamplighting and Georgia on My Mind

few applicants for an occupation which, in modern parlance, entailed unsocial hours and exposure to a variety of unpleasant climatic conditions.

Before taking the King's shilling, however, I had to undergo a medical examination. Towards the end of it the medical officer presented me with a beaker containing a mysterious fluid and invited me to sniff the fumes emanating therefrom. He then asked me what they reminded me of. 'Pears', I said. It was the correct answer. The purpose of the test was to ensure that potential lamplighters could detect the smell of gas.

I would be working in Paddington, where I lived. On the Monday following my medical I reported to the local depot in Edgware Road. I had bicycled there on a second-hand machine purchased a couple of days earlier. A grey-haired man in overalls gave me a rough summary of the various tasks I would have to perform in my new occupation.

Each lamplighter was allotted 200 lamps, all of them equipped with a clock and a pilot light. In lamps of a normal size four mantles hung in a circle below an enamel reflector. (A mantle is described in Chambers dictionaries thus: 'A hood or network of refractory material that becomes incandescent when exposed to a flame'). Two adjustable metal bands were attached to the face of the clocks. One of them lighted the lamp by turning on a gas tap while the other turned the tap off. An hour or so after sunrise I would have to bicycle round my 'patch' with my ladder and turn out lamps that had stayed on owing to a defective clock. In the evening the opposite procedure was observed. Monday, Tuesday and Wednesday mornings would be devoted to maintenance work: cleaning glass windows and enamel reflectors, replacing tattered or blackened mantles with new ones, oiling clocks and so on. The work was more or less evenly divided between two weeks. On Thursday and Friday mornings all the clocks had to be re-set and wound up. Broken windows, clogged pipes in the column of a lamp, faulty clocks etc were the responsibility of another department. As a member of a team of six lamplighters I would have to report every evening to our foreman outside a pub in Westbourne Park Villas an hour before official lighting-up time. These assemblages were known as musters. I would have to give him a form containing details of the day's work and of any repair jobs. Having completed my round I would have to return to base and write out another report. Finally my instructor gave me a list of the lamps in my charge and the streets, squares and so forth in which they were situated.

Having picked up my tool kit I met my foreman, Cassam, who was presently to supervise my fledgling efforts to ride my bicycle with a 20-foot extending ladder on my shoulder. He was a bulky, moon-faced man of about fifty. He had squinting eyes that lurked morosely behind heavy lenses. He had an air of calm truculence. 'Let's see 'ow yer shipes up then', he said.

Outside in the yard he shouldered a whopping big ladder, mounted his bicycle and bade me follow him. We eventually reached a quiet Victorian square in Bayswater where he came to a halt. 'It's all your'n', he said as he disencumbered himself of the ladder. I pushed my right shoulder through a space between two rungs in the middle of the ladder whose entire weight I then assumed. My burden was appallingly heavy. (In time I developed a callous on this shoulder). It seemed impossible at first to ride my bicycle without overbalancing and risking a fall. After half-an-hour of trial and error, however, I was pedalling around the square like a jousting knight, albeit not too jauntily. Cassam seemed satisfied with my little display. 'Don't be lite fer the muster ternite', he said as he clumped towards his bicycle.

The pub in question was called the Westbourne Arms. I reported for duty that evening to find several lamplighters standing around exchanging genial insults in a cobbled yard which was bounded by the pub, a vast coal dump and a brick wall overlooking railway tracks. I heard a steam train roaring past and saw white clouds hovering above the wall. Cassam was studying a form and waggling a cigarette in his mouth. As I approached him he said: 'Pick up yer tool bag and come darn wiv me'. There was a locker in a corner of the yard, which he unpadlocked with great solemnity. 'Stick these in yer bag', he said. He gave me six boxes of matches, a tin of lubricating oil, half-a-dozen pilot stems complete with porcelain teats, a roll of scrim and a piece of chamois leather. 'Look after yer shammy', he said, '''cos they only issues 'em once a year. And annuver fing. Don't wiste yer matches. If anybody asks yer fer a loit don't give 'em one'. Then he handed me two boxes of mantles, one of them marked Large and the other Bijou.

A jaunty little man marched down to the locker whistling a perky tune. He wore a weather-stained trilby, a shiny double-breasted suit, a tieless shirt and scuffed brown shoes. This was Bert. 'Give us a box of Beejews, guv', he said. 'Wot, annuver one?', exclaimed Cassam. 'Oi only gives yer one three diys ago'. (There was still a number of houses in Paddington that were lit by gas and so a bent lamplighter could earn a little on the side by selling mantles at cut prices). 'The bloomin' kids cloimbs up the lamps in the diytoim and nicks 'em, don't they?', retorted Bert in aggrieved tones. 'Oi don't know wot yer does wiv 'em', grumbled Cassam as he shoved a box of Bijous at Bert.

Cassam kept consulting his heavy pocket watch and finally

shouted: 'Let's 'ave yer'. He accompanied me as I bicycled round my lamps and came to my rescue when I ran into difficulties. To his obvious disgust it took me several days to get the hang of things.

I had 10 lamps in Westbourne Grove which were about 50 feet high. Their square lanterns, furnished with a dozen large mantles, hung from an arm overlooking the road. Bert also had 10 similar lamps in the Grove. We would meet once a week to clean the windows of his lanterns and so forth and on the following week meet to tackle my lot. We received extra payment for our additional work. The lanterns were winched down to shoulder level or, rather, to the level of Bert's shoulder. One of us would do the winching while the other stood in the middle of the road wielding a red flag.

I felt self-conscious in my role of lamplighter but especially so when I worked at ground level as I did in the Grove. To make matters worse Bert turned into a stentorian Cheekie Chappie on those occasions, greeting passers-by with such verbal felicities as 'It's all agony, Oivy' or 'Ow's yer love loif, darlin'?' or 'Woi don't yer git yer 'air cut 'enery?' He also gave raucous renditions of 'naughty' tunes like, for instance, 'If You Knew Susie Like I Knew Susie'. During our tea breaks in a local caff, however, he was oddly taciturn, stonewalling all my attempts to get a conversation going.

At a muster one evening a week or so after I had started the job, Cassam took me aside and said: 'Mr Lochness is piying 'is munfly visit ternoit. 'Es an inspector of public loiting so don't let 'im foind any of yer loits 'art.' Then he added darkly: 'Yer won't see 'im but he'll see you – 'cos 'es in a car.' I had a vision of a powerful, sinister figure prowling the streets in a sleek black limousine. I did actually set eyes on him eventually. However he turned out to be a timid, bespectacled little man whose car was indeed black but exceedingly ordinary. He was known inevitably as the Loch Ness Monster

It grieves me to admit that I was not a very conscientious lamplighter. The glass in my lamps tended to be smeary, few of my lights shone with dazzling intensity and my morning rounds were often conducted at a disgracefully late hour. Indeed, on Sunday mornings when I was usually clobbered with a hangover I did not turn out at all. And then there was my appalling handwriting. 'Oi can't mike 'ead nor tile of yer bloomin' 'Ong Kong wroiting', Cassam would grumble as he puzzled over one of my forms covered with wild scribbles. I began to combine maintenance work with resetting and winding up clocks, which I managed to get away with. I suspect that most of my fellow lamplighters skived as much as I did, or possibly even more so. 'It's me wot's 'olding the can', Cassam would tell an errant lamplighter. 'It's me the 'eads 'ave on the carpet up there when yer don't study yer lamps'.

I was something of a menace with my ladder when it rested on my shoulder for I had a habit of concentrating on the front half and forgetting about the remainder of it. As a result I occasionally clumped a passer-by with the rear end. Vigorous protests ensued, 'Mind them bleedin' steps', for instance or 'I say, matey, do try to control that beastly ladder of yours', or 'Bloody hell!'. Actually I do not think I scored more than three or four hits, none of whom, happily, suffered anything worse than a temporary increase of blood pressure. One rainy morning the hooks of my ladder savaged an umbrella belonging to a middle-aged Italian woman. She unleashed on me a torrent of abuse in fractured English. I offered to pay for the repair of the umbrella or even buy her a new one but she appeared not to hear what I was saying. 'I tell my beeg brother', she screeched. 'He come down 'ere and you be vairy sorry'. Then she marched off muttering imprecations. But the 'beeg brother' never materialised.

I was also something of a menace to myself. There were five or six tall lamps in Porchester Road with large glass bowls. One of them failed to light one night owing to a defective pilot light. To save a couple of seconds I inserted a lighted match into the ventilation hole at the base of the gas-filled bowl. A moment later – BOOM. However, both the bowl and myself survived the explosion. But I did not repeat the experiment. All lamps, apart from the tallest ones, had metal bars over which we hooked our ladder before climbing it. However, again to save a couple of seconds, I used merely to prop my ladder against the column of a lamp before my ascent. This was imprudent at the best of times but on winter days when pavements were caked with ice it was positively insane. On such a day I propped my ladder against a lamp in a side street and began to mount it. Suddenly the ladder made a lightening descent to the ground. I lay on top of the ladder for a few moments with my nose pressed against a sheet of ice. Then I rose shakily to my feet, the victim merely of a slight state of shock. I had learnt another lesson. One morning, feeling inordinately bored and irritated, I slammed the hooks of my ladder over the metal bar of a lamp with extreme violence. This caused a pane of glass to jump out of its frame and shatter on my head. Blood began to trickle down my face. I padlocked my ladder, bestrode my bicycle and pedalled for all I was worth to St Mary's Hospital in Harrow Road. A nurse in the casualty ward examined the wound. I asked her anxiously how many stitches I would need. She merely laughed and said that a strip of elastoplast would do the job.

My ancient bicycle gave me a great deal of trouble. Had I possessed a modicum of sense I would have saved up to buy a new sturdy model or obtained one on the never-never. The worn tyres frequently acquired punctures, the rarely oiled chain creaked arthritically as it revolved, a link snapped from time to time, and the brakes gave up the ghost eventually. Punctures I could deal with, otherwise I took my machine to a local bicycle shop for repairs.

In time, however, the owner of the shop found himself doing a great deal of repair work on motor bikes, which were then becoming popular. He eventually declined to waste his time on a silly old push bike that was only fit for a scrap heap. As a consequence I found myself pedalling around with non-functioning brakes. I would bring my machine to a halt by bouncing the top of my ladder on the surface of the road, a somewhat precarious operation. When I was not carrying my ladder I used my right leg instead.

One evening I was greeted by the spectacle of a lamp on fire in one of my streets in a working-class area off Harrow Road. Blue and orange flames fed by gas from a leaking pipe in the column of the lamp leapt wickedly around a twisted lantern whose shattered glass littered the pavement below. I rang the Board's Emergency Services from a telephone box nearby. I was told that two engineers would be sent down to tackle the fire and that I should stand by the lamp in the meantime. I did as instructed feeling a trifle apprehensive. A handful of children had gathered on the opposite pavement and were clearly enjoying the show.

One morning in another street in the same neighbourhood I had just descended from a lamp with a defective clock when I was confronted by a little boy who stared at me wide-eyed for a moment or two. Then he said: 'Are you Robin Hood, mister?' With the greatest reluctance I told him that I was not the illustrious gentleman in question. Had I answered in the affirmative, though, he might well have boasted later to older children that he had met the famous outlaw and been subjected to hurtful taunts.

I contracted one of my numerous punctures one morning and was trudging disconsolately along a street off the Harrow Road when a band of children began marching behind me chanting:

'We won the war-ah in nineteen forty four-ah
'We won the war-ah in nineteen forty four-ah.
This raised my spirits somewhat.

I had to tend several massive pretentiously ornate lamps outside Porchester Hall, where banquets, public meetings and bazaars were frequently held. One evening I was climbing my ladder to light one of these lamps when I noticed groups of people in evening dress standing around near the entrance of the hall. A mingled smell of cigar smoke and perfume was in the air. A banquet was obviously about to take place. As I plodded past the entrance I heard a woman call out my name. I turned to find myself confronted by my sister in an evening gown and her dinner-jacketed husband. I became painfully aware of my shabby working clothes, the 20-foot extending ladder on my shoulder and my battered old bicycle. They gaped at me for a moment and then, to their great credit, they succumbed to fits of helpless laughter.

Shortly before the start of my career as a lamplighter Hal Woolf achieved the rare distinction of getting the sack. He had been a member of Cassam's team. He used to regard the evening round as something to be enjoyed as much as possible. It was mid-summer after all and the weather was clement. Having completed half his round or thereabouts he would drop into a pub for half-a-bitter, which he would imbibe in a relaxed leisurely fashion. Sometimes the view from the top of his ladder would please him greatly, a bombed site, for instance, overgrown with flowers and exotic weeds, or a spectacularly roseate sunset. In that case he would roll a joint, i.e. a cigarette consisting of a mixture of tobacco and hemp, and then inhale it slowly as he luxuriated in the visual splendours before him. After the last lamplighter but one had departed for home Cassam often hung around for half-an-hour or more before Hal put in an appearance. This did not endear him to Cassam.

One evening Hal emerged from his alcoholic half-way-house and came face to face with Cassam. 'Wot are yer doin' in a pub when yer ought to be loiting yer lamps?' demanded Cassam. 'I popped in to buy a box of matches', said Hal. 'It don't tike nobody a quarter-of-an-hour to buy a box of matches', commented Cassam sourly. Two days later Hal managed to lose his ladder. This proved to be the last straw and he was given his marching orders.

Many artists about this time followed Hal's example and took up lamplighting. The *Daily Express* published an article on the phenomenon which was accompanied by a photograph of a painter/lamplighter standing at the top of a ladder and peering solemnly into a lantern.

Tony Kingsmill, a member of this redoubtable breed later settled down on a Greek island, where he devoted himself entirely to painting. (He even sold his work). On his first night as a lamplighter he spotted an unlit lamp on a derelict yard in a poor neighbourhood of Paddington. As he was hooking his ladder to the lamp a brick whistled past his head. It seems that a prostitute was at work in a dark corner of the yard and that her enraged customer had taken direct action. Tony offered apologies for interrupting their business but insisted that he had a job to do. This they grudgingly accepted. On the following evening, and on subsequent ones, Tony would announce his presence in the yard by shouting: 'Lamplighter coming. Lamplighter coming'.

The Last Lamplighter

'Short-Arse' Charlie was a wizened little Scot with bandy legs, who had a reputation for 'telling' on his mates to Cassam. All his lamps were of a normal size. When it was merely a question of turning on or turning off a lamp he would scorn to use his ladder and instead scramble up the column of the lamp like a monkey. Al Paget, large, slow-moving and well-dressed, affected a cool, nonchalant attitude to his job. Indeed, he gave the impression that he was only doing it for the fresh air and the exercise and that his mind was on higher matters. Actually, his mind was on greyhound racing. He claimed to have a fool-proof system for beating the tote. But if this had been the case he would hardly have been working as a lamplighter. He bought Cassam a 20-pocket of Woodbines every week. They were sweeteners which ensured that Cassam turned a blind eye to his skiving. Bill was an obsessive teetotaller. 'Nivver drink lalcolol', he would urge me frequently. 'It rots the soles of yer boots, mite'. One of my predecessors used to ride around with a huge alarm clock hanging from his handle bars. In truth he was a little simpleminded. One morning he picked up a glass bowl at the store in Edgeware Road. Cassam happened to be standing around in the yard. He asked the foreman how he should carry the bowl while riding his bicycle. 'Put it over yer bloomin' 'ead', said Cassam. The simple fellow gingerly lowered the bowl over his head and bicycled away.

The years rolled past but I failed to blossom as a jazz trumpeter owing to my lack of talent for improvisation. But I could knock out a tune on my instrument either by ear or from written music. I practised scales and arpeggios every day with dogged persistence. For a time I played a cornet in an amateur brass band which, however, did not afford me much satisfaction. I sat in with an amateur dance band for two sessions but could not keep up with the other musicians.

Lamplighting and Georgia on My Mind

I was plainly going nowhere. Nevertheless stupid obstinacy prevented me from throwing in the sponge. I should have taken to the streets with my trumpet but, surprisingly enough, it did not occur to me to do so at the time. Buskers had not yet become respectable and this would have appealed to my bohemian instincts.

One afternoon I was marching resolutely up and down arpeggios in various keys when a neighbour of mine, who worked at night, flung open his window and bellowed like a mad bull. I took the hint and called it a day. There was a chicken coop in a garden nearby whose inhabitants included two cocks. Whenever I hit the high register they burst into an ear-splitting duet. High notes also caused a mongrel dog in another garden to howl like a soul in hell. I once apologised for my trumpeting efforts to an occupant, a middle-aged actor, of the flat below. He said he found the scales and arpeggios a bit of a bore but enjoyed my melodic effusions. However what tended to get him down were, as he put it, my musical appreciation noises. He meant the singing, shouting and stamping I occasionally indulged in when carried away by stirring music, usually of a symphonic nature, on my radio or record player.

Once a week a young African, who was also studying the trumpet, used to visit me to borrow my instrument. It was a superior model to his own and he liked to luxuriate in its golden tones. Tall and exceedingly black, he had an open smiling face. He worked as a messenger for some firm or other in Fitzrovia. His invariable greeting was: 'Hiya prof'. He never ceased to remind me that his favourite 'jazz horn' was Howard McGee. 'Howard McGee's my man', he would say with a dreamy expression. 'I really dig that cat'. He eventually joined a semi-pro Latin-American band.

A 16-year old ex-Borstal boy, the son of a friend of mine,

The Last Lamplighter

used to drop in sometimes to listen to my jazz records. One day he told me he wanted to learn to play the trumpet. I lent him my instrument so that he could get started. Sadly he pawned it and sold the pawn ticket. I chose not to go to the police over the matter.

Shortly afterwards I gave up lamplighting. However, I used to amuse myself with a fantasy in which I continued to pursue this noble occupation and in time became the Last Lamplighter. Decorated by the Queen and deferentially interviewed by high-ranking journalists, I achieved lasting fame in the form of a statue in an important London square.

POSTSCRIPT, 1999

I continue to plunge into the Soho melee most nights and usually find it an enjoyable experience. My favourite haunt is the French, which has not changed essentially over the years, though non-regulars tend of an evening to outnumber regulars. This was not the case in the old days when the French was almost like a club.

Soho, however, has changed a great deal in the last thirty years. During the 60s there was a proliferation of striptease clubs and pornographic book shops which had a depressing effect on the village. There was certainly little fun and gaiety to be found in strip joints, where the gloomy spectators could not even bring themselves to applaud the acts. On a notable occasion I was watching a turn in one of these clubs when the artiste brought her gyrations to an abrupt halt to stare at us contemptuously for a few moments. Then she shouted: 'Why are you all looking so bloody miserable?' Answer was there none.

In the following decade, however, many strip joints closed while Westminster Council decreed that the number of pornographic book shops in Soho should be limited to ten. In the 80s boutiques began to establish themselves in the heart

The Last Lamplighter

of Soho but Black Wednesday saw them off. I have to admit I did not shed many tears over their demise. The 80s also saw the emergence of Mass Gaiety in parts of Soho. (Most homosexuals I know deplored this phenomenon.)

In the early 90s there was an eruption of restaurants, cafés and bars. Tables and chairs on the pavement outside most of these establishments gave Soho a Parisian air. Before long, however, the area became a magnet for young suburbanites who now launch a mass invasion on Friday and Saturday evenings. In the streets there is an atmosphere of feverish excitement – Sohomania? – and a great deal of shouting and horseplay. Anyone drunk and silly enough can hire a rickshaw for a jaunt around Soho streets, some of which have been pedestrianised.

What I would have once referred to as bohemian Soho continues to survive against all odds, though in an attenuated form. But I miss, of course, the old faces. It would be nice to hear again MacBryde singing sub voce an old Scotch air or Archer declaring he was absolutely furious about something or other. And I would give a lot to be under Bryce MacNabb's hat again – well, for about half-an-hour I suppose.